The Internet Sucks-Here's How to Use It Safely

How to Stay Safe on Today's Internet

Ken Baker

ISBN:1523956143
ISBN-13:9781523956142

DEDICATION

I never know what to say here. I didn't really get any help on the book, but thanks to my family and friends.

CONTENTS

Even if you follow all of my suggestions, it is still **possible** to get infected with a virus or malware, or have online accounts compromised in some way, or have other security issues. The bad guys are highly motivated by $, and come up with new attacks every day – faster than anyone can block or come up with new tips.
So reading this book does not offer any guarantee that nothing bad will happen to the reader on the internet.

Keep informed and educated.

ACKNOWLEDGMENTS

I got some information from various internet sources.
https://googleonlinesecurity.blogspot.com/2015/07/new-research-comparing-how-security.html
GRC.com
Microsoft.com
Amazon.com
Google.com
Yahoo.com
Norton.com
AVG.com
Dropbox.com
Avast.com
Torproject.org
Sandboxie.com

All images taken and edited by me.
All the tips / suggestions in this book are explained in easy to use terms by me (Ken Barker). Many are common security practices and can be found in other sources. The tips I offer as exclusive to this book (or my web site) where thought of by me and are not available from any other sources – as far as I know.

Introduction

Unfortunately just having an antivirus program isn't enough to protect you from the bad ad's, pop ups, and malware that infect most computers today.
YOU have to have an idea of what is good and bad.
YOU have to know what to click on and what not to click on.
YOU have to know when to say "OK" to a pop up message and when to close the message box.

Unfortunately YOU have to protect YOURSELF.

Unfortunately security and convenience do not go together.

Being safe on the internet today takes a little work.

Everyone needs to have a basic literacy on computer usage and how to protect yourself online.

I am writing this book because I have seen so many people get infected with a virus or malware and they don't know how it happened. They have an antivirus program like *Norton* installed and it still happens.

Today's internet is filled with pop-up ads, programs that get installed without you knowing about it, and fake warnings that trick you into paying a scammer for help and costing you several hundred dollars because the computer is not usable.

So many people have said they don't know what to do when they see these messages. They're scared to click on things but there also scared to close things there not sure about.

You need to take proactive steps to stop this stuff from happening to you.

I will show you how to protect yourself and what to know to keep this from happening to you.

I try to keep each tip and chapter short enough as to not seem overwhelming, but still provide you with what you need to know.

One of the first things I tell people about using a computer is:

Don't be afraid of the computer - or in this case - of clicking (or not clicking) things.

(Almost) nothing you do can't be undone.

With a little bit of knowledge you will know what to do when you see things pop up on the internet; and hopefully even keep it from happening.

I will give you step by step instructions for most things with pictures. Giving you the confidence to do them, even if you think you cant.
* Sometimes things change after this book is published or the steps are slightly different for some users, but if the steps are not exact they should be close enough for you to look at the screen and know what to do.

Most of the time I am assuming you already have a computer set up and have been using it for a while. All of the information in the book can be used for a new computer setup if you are starting with a new one.

Most of the information is good no matter how you surf the web. It is written mostly with a Windows PC in mind with the step by step direction. But whether you use a computer (PC or Mac), tablet, or phone the Information is universal.

There are a couple of tips in this book that you won't find anywhere else!
These are tips that I discovered either by my own experience or while helping some of my customers over the past 10+ years.

I suggest reading the full chapter or even the full book before following the suggestions I offer. Then going back and start making the changes you need.

Each chapter ends with a Recommendation, a summation of the work needed, the difficulty, and the need for most people to do it.

The difficulty is a scale of 1-3. Essentially - easy, a little work, and a little harder. Most of them are easy. The ones that are a little harder most people don't need to do them. They are to let you know about them if you feel the need.

The need also has 3 categories. Do, should do, and can do.
Of course, the suggestions marked as "Do" are things everyone should do as a minimum to protect yourself.
Chapter 30 lists the most important ones everyone should look into.

1 BACKUP YOUR FILES

Backing up your files is not really an internet security issue, but backing up your files is the most important thing you should do as a computer user.

Even with everything moving to the internet these days most people have music, work or other documents, and PHOTOS on their computer. They may not get printed up anymore, but PHOTOS are the most important thing to most people. Since they are not being printed, you need to have backups.

If you do get infected with something nasty (yes, it can happen even if you do everything I suggest in this book) or your computer crashes, you will be soooooooo upset if you lose your 49 page report, wedding photos, or pictures of your kids growing up.

I can't tell you how many times I've started working on someone's computer and seen the "oh no" face when I tell them their hard drive crashed or they were infected with something and they did not have a backup, had to pay extra to have a backup done, or pay a lot to have the drive sent away for data recovery because they did not do a backup.

You know what almost all of them said after they calmed down? "I was going to do it…….." Yep.

I've heard someone in the photography / video business say;
"If there aren't 3 copies of it, - it does not exist".

That may sound excessive at first, but something can quit easily happen to any 2 copies of a file you have. That's an original on the computer and 1 backup.

Your computer and your backup drive can burn in a fire (hope not).
USB sticks, external hard drives, and yes CD/DVD's do go bad.
Of course virus' can infect your computer AND your 1 backup.
Things get stolen.
You or someone else accidently erased your backup.

Everyone loses data somehow. It's a question of when, not if.

Having three copies (2 backups) of your files is the standard suggestion from any computer expert. One (1) of those should be someplace other than your home. It's called an "off-site backup". As stated above, if there is a fire, you can lose everything at the same time. No matter how many copies you have there.

Some people (or companies) physically take one of their backups to another location such as a friend's house.

With the internet taking everything else over, why shouldn't it take over this too.

There are several online backup companies you can use. You can use free online storage provided by Google, Microsoft, Apple, or Amazon. One of these you almost certainly have access to.

First, I'll talk about the traditional backup.

This is putting the file or files you want backed up onto a CD/DVD, USB stick, or an external hard drive. It all works. It will depend on you and how much data you have to backup.

1. Your computer or your antivirus software, such as Norton, may bug you about backing up your computer. Windows and some antivirus programs have a backup program built in. Just click on that reminder icon in the lower right corner and follow the steps. Or you can click on the Start button and type "backup". You will see the shortcut to set up Windows Backup.

Windows 10 Start button

> If you're using an antivirus to do the backup and you
> know you're going to keep their service, go ahead. You
> just need to specify where you want to files to go. Also
> know that **you will need their software to get the files
> back**. So if you ever go away from that antivirus, you'll
> need to download their backup software separately.

Be sure you're going to a CD/DVD or USB drive. Norton and the other antivirus programs often want you to store the files online. Online backup is great, see further down, but they give you limited space and you may need to pay for more. I would make a hard copy first.

Another issue that I have seen is the backup programs will store their backup on a D: drive that the manufacturer provided as a backup of Windows if you run them and don't have an external USB or hard drive plugged in. You do not want to use this D: for anything.

Let's assume you are starting from scratch.

Backing up to a drive:

I would suggest not using CD/DVD's unless you have to. Many new laptop and desktop computers don't have DVD drives any more. USB drives or external hard drives have taken over the storage market. USB sticks are often on sale for around $10 that will backup up to 32 Gigabytes of information. 32 Gigabytes is a good amount. Documents are very small, and if you don't have 1000's of photos or videos, that could be enough. But a good backup drive can be reused and store multiple copies so I suggest larger drives or external hard drives. External hard drives can be on sale for $60-$90 that will hold a Terabyte of information. This should be enough for most anyone reading this book.

You can check to see how much storage you need: Open your file browser so you see "My Computer" or "Computer" or "This PC", depending on what version of Windows you have. Click on that so you see the hard drives of your computer like C: and D: and so on. Right click on the C: then click on "properties" at the bottom of the menu. Here you can see how much space your computer is using. You can use that as a way to see how large a drive you need to back up to. When you look at that "used space" keep in mind a lot of that is the operating system and programs. You will not need the full amount of space that is "used". This just gives you an idea of a minimum amount of pace to look for in a hard drive.

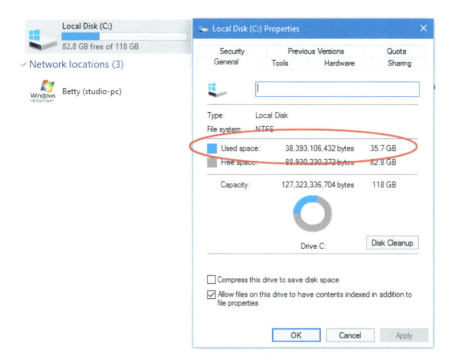

2. You could also just "copy and paste" the files and folders you want to back up from your documents folders to the new USB or external hard drive.

3. The external hard drive should have its own backup software. It should run the first time you plug in the external hard drive. So pay attention to any pop ups when you first use an external hard drive. (from chapter 15) Since **you just plugged in the drive** and **you do want to run their software**, follow their prompts to set up the backup.

Example of Western Digital hard drive software prompt.

After you set up the backup, make sure it works. It should put an icon in the lower right corner of your computer so you can see it working. The first backup could take several hours.

Tip: Also look at the files on the drive the next day to make sure it did copy what you want.

I have had people bring in their backup drives for me to restore their files, and when we look at it – its empty. They just assumed it worked and never looked at it.

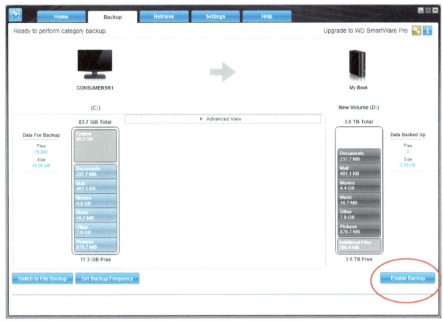

Make sure backup is turned on.

There is other 3rd party software you can use to run the backup if you like. I have used one of the online backup companies software called Crashplan (Crashplan.com) to back up to an external hard drive for free.

Online file backup:

As I mentioned doing things online has taken over almost everything, backup is no exception.

I also mentioned you may be able to back up your computer with free storage provided by Google, Microsoft, Apple, or Amazon. If you have an account with any of these companies – I'm sure you do – you can use their web site or a program to upload your files to them. Their online storage services are:

Google Drive
Microsoft One Drive
Apple iCloud

Amazon Prime (free unlimited photo storage)

There are also other popular sites you can use for free storage. You may have heard of Dropbox; it is the most popular file backup, storage, and sharing site. There is also Shutterfly and Flickr. The last two are photo backup sites.

Dropbox.com
Shutterly.com
Flickr.com

The free options usually have limited space, around 5 Gigabytes. Other backup software or sites are available for a price. The services mentioned so far have paid versions for more space.

The sites that specialize in online backup are Carbonite.com, Crashplan.com, Box.com, Sugarsync.com, and more.

Carbonite is the oldest (2006) site dedicated to backup and they are still around and trusted by many large companies and people.

You can check into each one of these and choose the one you like. PC Magazine and other sites have done reviews you can look up.

I have used all the services I have mentioned so far except Box.com. Since this chapter is mostly about straight backup, I will recommend Carbonite or Crashplan for online backup and Google, Microsoft, Apple, Dropbox, or Amazon services for smaller file storage.

If you can, put your important files as many places as you can. Just in case….

All of these sites and program are secure and encrypted. Create a good strong password when you sign up (chapter 8). They also work with Mac, Android, and iOS.

* Special TiP: Don't leave your external hard drive plugged in all the time. It can back up an infection or get encrypted by a new type of virus called *ransomware- Cryptolocker*. (See chapter 19 for more info on this type of virus.) Just plug in the backup drive when you need to run the backup. This can be once a week or once a month. (or how often you like. Daily if you think you add enough to your computer.)

***

Recommendation: Backup your files!

The Work: Setup your computers backup, or another backup to a USB or external hard drive as well as an online backup site.

Difficulty: 2

The Need: DO IT NOW!   No, not later.   NOW!

I will remind you several times through the book.

2 PUT A PASSWORD ON YOUR COMPUTER

As a security related book, I would be remiss if I did not mention the importance of having a password on your computer (account / user name), and keeping the password to yourself. Even though it is not needed for internet security, you should practice basic computer security too. It's like - not keeping the keys in the ignition of your car. You really don't want just anybody to be able to get on your computer.

When you first set up your computer, you are asked for a *"User Name"* (or email address). This creates the *user account* that can set your experience apart from other users of the same computer. That's easy enough, but what a lot of people don't do is the next step –, **put a password on the account**.

WARNING: With windows 8 and 10, Microsoft wants you to use a Microsoft email as your log in. I strongly recommend **NOT DOING THIS**. This process lets you access Microsoft services and sync information between computers, but for most people I believe it causes more problems and can turn into a security issue or loss of information if the user ever needs to take their computer to someone to have work done, or forgets the email or password.

Even if you are the only person using the computer, you should have a password. If someone else ever does use the computer they can use it without being able to access your desktop, web browser, and personal files. *if you do setup a user account with an email address, your password for the email and user account are the same.

If nothing else having a password on your computer can keep someone who breaks into your house or steals your computer from being able to access that stuff easily.

You can easily create another account for someone or turn on the built in "Guest" account. These accounts can be removed or turned off just as easy.

I would suggest not letting family members use your account or know your password. It turns out a lot of identity theft is done by family members or people you know.

This is key if you have kids or someone else using the computer you don't want to install stuff without your permission.

The password you put on the computer does not have to be as hard as your online passwords, but you don't want to make it something easy like child or pet names that anyone can guess. Make it unique and something only you know.

You will also have to protect it by making sure kids or whoever doesn't watch you type it in. At home this is difficult because people are often right beside each other and watching what you do.

On Phones or tablets having a good password can be key to keeping people (your kids) from buying apps or spending money in apps. On phones you should have 2 "passwords". First the account / email that you have setup the phone with has a password, and second you should have a pin, diagram, or if possible fingerprint set up to access the lock screen.

Since phone / tablets are becoming the main computer for many people and has so much personal information like apps that can do banking as well as contacts, email, and photos... you need to protect them even more because they are also so easily lost or stolen.

If you are setting up a new computer with Windows 8 or 10 follow these steps to create an account without a Microsoft email:

*On the **Sign in to your PC screen**, where it asks for your email address, move down to the bottom of the screen and find:*

*"**Sign in without a Microsoft account?**" link on the lower left of the screen and click it. Then click on "**Local account**" button on the lower right of the next screen.*

This will allow you to create a normal User Name or Local Account

If you need to add a password to your current account:

Click on the Start button in the lower left corner > type the word "user" > in the search results that show, click on "User Accounts" (sub title "control panel").

Now you see the "Make changes to your account" window. You should see your user name and icon to the right, and some links on the left.

Windows 8 and 10 users: One of those links should be "Make changes to my account in Pc Settings". Click on that link. Now click on "Sign-in options" on the left menu pane. Here you will see different password options such as create a password, PIN, and Picture password. Chose "create a password" to add a password to your account. You need to have a password set before you can create a PIN or Picture password.

Windows 7 users: simply click the "Create a password" link to add the password.

***

Recommendation: Put a password on your user account at setup or add one now.

The Work: Putting a password on your account.

Difficulty: 2

The Need: Do

3 CREAT A STANDARD USER ACCOUNT

When you first set up your computer, the username you create is given full authority to install programs and do anything on a computer. This is called an "Administrator" account. This is nice and easy for you. It also makes it easier for virus and malware to get installed on your computer. The way some of these programs are installed from the web, they don't need any special permission if you are an Administrator. They can just install behind your back and you don't know it until it's too late.

Web sites today rely on small programs called *scripts*. Your web browser runs these scripts when a page loads. They make Facebook, YouTube, and most every site work the way it does today. They make Facebook update posts and YouTube suggest other videos.

Usually scripts don't have the ability to install a program on your computer. But now the bad guys have found a way to make the web browser install their malware in a way that does not need any special permission if your user account is an administrator.

A "Standard" user is an account that can do most of what people do on a computer like surf the web but can't do things like install programs or even run some programs without the "permission" of and Administrator account by typing their password.

This chapter's suggestion is a common security practice. You probably have a user name and password for work. With them you can run what you need to do your job, but may not be able to install new software or a printer.

If you have been using your computer for a while, this is one of those things that I mentioned in the Introduction that takes a little work; and the way some of these bad programs are installing, it may have less impact than in the past. But if you are someone who has had problems with multiple infections or are getting scared of what is out there this is a good step to take.

I will walk you through creating a new user account, and making it an Administrator, then turn your account into a Standard user so you won't lose your desktop, files, or web favorites. You will keep using your computer they way you always have but when you install something you will be prompted for the password from the other account.

If you get this prompt for the other accounts password and you don't know why or how it came up. DON'T PUT IT IN. That's a sign that something is trying to run that you don't know about.

This is the hardest suggestion to do in the book if you are working with an existing computer because it requires multiple steps. Read the full chapter before coming back and following along with the steps.

Creating a Standard User Account in Windows 8 or 10:

Click on the Start button in the lower left corner > type the word "user" > in the search results that show, click on "User Accounts" (sub title "control panal").

Now you see the "Make changes to your account" window. You should see your user name and icon to the right, and some links on the left. Look to see if "Administrator" or "Local Administrator" is under your user name. One of those links to the left should be "Manage another account". Click on that link.

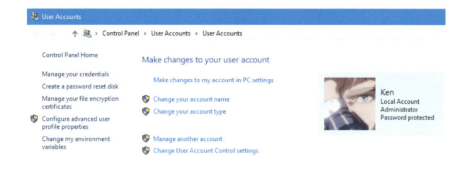

This is the "Choose the user you would like to change" page. Again you see your user name and icon. Below the section box, there should be a link for "Add a new user in PC settings". Click on that link.

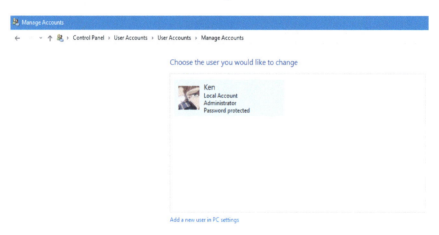

A new window opens for "Accounts", and hopefully "Family & other users" is highlighted on the left pane. If not, click on it.

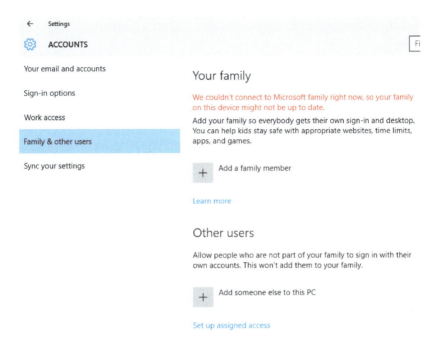

In the main window under the section "Other users", click on the + "Add someone else to this PC".

(Microsoft wants everyone to sign in with an email but we don't want that)
Click on "I don't have this persons sign-in information". It will ask you to create an account. We don't want that either; so click on "Add a user without a Microsoft Account" link at the bottom.

Now enter a user name like "user" or "Admin" – short for Administrator. Enter a password and a password hint. Click Next.

If you have Windows 8, your account has turned into a "Standard user" and you should be done.

Now you will see the new user name in the *Other users* section. It is a standard user by default. Click on it and the area around it turns grey. There are now 2 buttons to *Change account type* or *Remove*. Click on *Change account type*. In the blue window that opens click in the drop down menu where it says "Standard User", and change it to "Administrator".

Creating a Standard User Account in Windows 7:

Click on the Start button in the lower left corner > type the word "user" > in the search results that show, click on "User Accounts".

Now you see the "Make changes to your account" window. You should see your user name and icon to the right, and some links on the left. Look to see if "Administrator" or "Local Administrator" is under your user name. If you are an Administrator one of those links to the left is "manage another account" click on that link. Now click on "Create a new account".

Now add a new user name and choose the "Administrator" radio button below. Click "next" to finish creating the account.

Now you will see that new user listed. Click on it to add a password. See Chapter 2 if you need help adding the password.

Now whenever something wants to install on your computer, you will be prompted to add the new users account password.

If **your** Account has not changed to a Standard user, then you need to go back to the User Accounts screen in step 1. Click on "change your account type", and choose the "Standard user" radio button then click the "Change Account Type" button to confirm.

***

Recommendation: Create an Administrator account and make your account a Standard user so you will be able to stop some virus & malware programs from installing on your computer without your knowledge.

The Work: This is probably the hardest thing to do in this book – creating a new account, making it an administrator, changing your current account to a standard user.

Difficulty: 3

The Need: Do

4 ANTIVIRUS & MALWARE PROTECTION

Everyone has been taught that you need antivirus protection on your computer, but top security advisors don't even list using an antivirus in the top 5 things to do. Their focus is on passwords and other practices – all of which I cover in this book.

I still recommend an antivirus program for most people because you still need their protection. But you also need to add an anti-malware program like *Malwarebytes* to your computer needs. And you may not need to buy an anti virus program like *Norton*.

Today a program that protects you from malware is probably more important than 3rd party antivirus software.

If it comes to not wanting to pay for 2 different programs to protect your computer, buy the malware protection and use one of the free antivirus programs. The malware protection is usually cheaper too.

Antivirus programs can't stop or remove most of the infections people get today because they came from the internet and you gave them permission somehow. And they are regular programs classified as MALWARE, not a VIRUS so *Norton / McAfee* would get sued if they started to block or remove them.

When I tell people that they have a virus, most of them would reply "how did this happen, I have an antivirus?" or "why am I paying for (insert favorite antivirus program here) ?"

You get malware on your computer much the same way as a virus. Although it rarely comes through email (with the exception of the new type of infections called ransomware). It is almost 100% from clicking on an ad on a web page or being tricked into downloading something you did not mean to install.

Even if you accidentally click on an ad on a web page while moving your mouse, it can install malware.

Often programs from the web don't need the same permission as installing from a CD.

Many web pages have their text turned into pop up links as ads, and just moving the mouse over them can cause some malware to be installed.

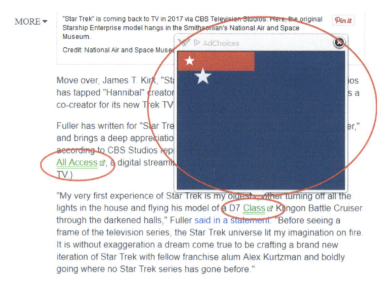

Move over, James T. Kirk, "Sta   ios
has tapped "Hannibal" creator   s a
co-creator for its new Trek TV

Fuller has written for "Star Tre   er,"
and brings a deep appreciatio
according to CBS Studios rep
All Access ☑, a digital streami
TV.)

"My very first experience of Star Trek is my oldest ... other turning off all the
lights in the house and flying his model of a D7 Class ☑ Klingon Battle Cruiser
through the darkened halls," Fuller said in a statement. "Before seeing a
frame of the television series, the Star Trek universe lit my imagination on fire.
It is without exaggeration a dream come true to be crafting a brand new
iteration of Star Trek with fellow franchise alum Alex Kurtzman and boldly
going where no Star Trek series has gone before."

These double underlined green words show pop-up ads in the middle of the page while you move your mouse over them. Making it easy to accidently click on an ad..

It's horrible!

The bad guys are just taking advantage of the way the internet works today.

The other chapters in this book will help you deal with these ads and other issues.

What do I do? You ask.
>   Answer: USE AN ANTI MALWARE PROGRAM
                 (and use chapter 7's suggestions)

For Malware protection, I recommend and use *Malwarebytes* found at Malwarebytes.org or possibly in stores like Staples and Best Buy. The paid version (about $30) will scan files and web sites as you use them and update automatically like antivirus programs do. THIS IS WHAT YOU WANT. It can prevent a lot of this stuff from getting on your computer.

The Free version needs to be manually updated and ran. So it can only remove things AFTER they get on your computer.

I have had it block or warn me about websites I have tried to visit, and I use the program to clean client's computers that I work on.

There are other anti-malware programs available, but I have not had good luck with them. Even the one that started the anti-malware business - *Spybot Search and Destroy* is not very good these days.

Since I still recommend an antivirus for most people…

For paid mainstream antivirus programs I like *Kaspersky* or *Norton* for the brand names you will find in the store, and *Avast, AVG, or Microsoft* for the free alternatives you will find online.
I do not like nor recommend *McAfee*.

AVG is one program that I have seen block some of the tools that I use to work on customers computers. These tools do sometimes work similar to virus or malware so that is good.

But in general I leave antivirus choice to the customer. Most people use what they know or what a friend, "who knows about computers", tells them to use.

Microsoft actually includes an antivirus / malware program called *Defender* built in to Windows 8 and 10 and one you could download from them called *Security Essentials* for Windows 7 and Vista. So you don't need to install any antivirus from another company.

The Microsoft antivirus has not gotten the best reviews through the years, but the most recent tests (as of January 2016) put it on par with the rest of the antivirus programs. And I have seen it block, warn, or remove some of the more serious threats that the others did not. Most notably I'm referring to the new big threat of malware called **Cryptolocker** that encrypts or scrambles your files unless you pay them several hundred dollars. Cryptolocker is part of a group of malware called **ransomware**. Windows Defender caught this before any of the other antivirus programs did.

I use the built in antivirus from Microsoft.

If you use Microsoft *Defender* or *Security Essentials* with *Malwarebytes* you should be fine. If you feel more secure with Norton or another antivirus program go ahead and install it.

***

Recommendations: Use *Malwarebytes* with the antivirus of your choice.

The Work: buying and installing malware protection, possibly installing an antivirus program also.

Difficulty: 1

The Need: Do

Malwarebytes – Malwarebytes.org or possibly found at local store like Staples or Best Buy.

AVG – AVG.com or possibly found at local store like Staples or Best Buy.

Avast – Avast.com or possibly found at local store like Staples or Best Buy.

Microsoft Defender – Comes with Windows 8 or 10. No need to install anything.

Microsoft Security Essentials – download from Microsoft.com for windows 7 or Vista.

5 KEEP YOUR COMPUTER & SOFTWARE UPDATED

Some of the main ways virus creators use to get into your computer is through "holes" that have been found in the operating system. and various software you use. The Operating System (OS) is what runs your computer, phone, or tablet. This includes Windows, Android and yes, Apples OS X and iOS too. Unfortunately some of the most common software is also the one with the most holes. Adobe Flash player and Adobe Reader have been two of the most attacked software titles out there – and everyone has them.

In chapter 4 I mentioned how security experts don't list using an antivirus in their top 5 things to do. They do list keeping your operating system and software up-to-date as the #1 thing to do.

So you need to keep your computer and software updated.

Usually programs and the operating system update automatically, but sometimes the updates get turned off or the user just closes or ignores the window asking them to authorize the update. This is why chapter 13 talked about paying attention to pop ups.

You should check your Operating systems update settings and make sure they are turned on and allow updates to software when they prompt you.

Windows updates:

For any current version of Windows (Vista,7,8,10*) click on your start button > type the words "Windows Update" > click on the Windows Update that showed up in the search results . Then on the left had menu, click on "Update settings" > make sure the drop down menu shows "automatic".

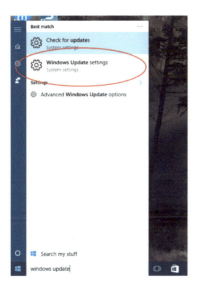

There are options for you to get updates and install them when prompted, but this is when people get in trouble and never install the updates. Automatic is the best option for anyone reading this book.

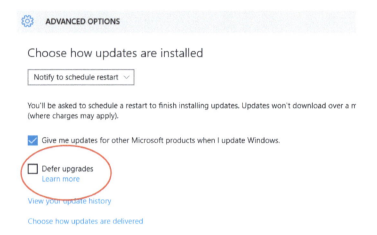

*Windows 10 updates can't be turned off, but they can be delayed (deferred). Make sure they are not deferred.

Mac OS X: Click on "System Preferences" > App Store. Make sure the check boxes for automatic updates are checked. There is a heading line and a couple sub lines to check.

Android and iOS: These update automatically and can't really be turned off, but need you to OK the installation.

Adobe software: Both *Flash* and *Reader* will update automatically. When they prompt you to do the update you need to make sure the check boxes allowing them to check and install updates is checked.

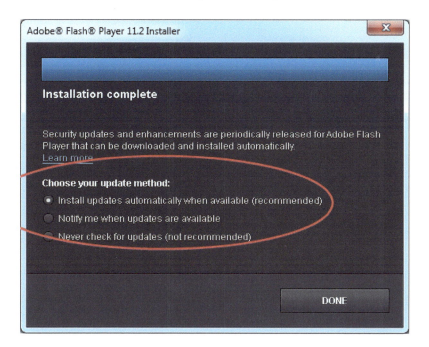

Java: Java is another program that everyone has and is often targeted. I talk about uninstalling or disabling Java in chapter 22. It is being phased out of modern web sites and you should not really need it. But if you still have it - Java gives you a small popup in the lower right corner when it is ready for an update. Then you get a prompt in the middle of the screen asking if you want to give this program permission to run. You see the java name and logo and should say "yes" to this prompt.

NEVER UPDATE SOFTWARE FROM A WEB PAGE! See chapter 13.

***

Recommendation: Keep your operating system and software up to date.

The Work: Checking to make sure updates are turned on, and allowing software updates when prompted.

Difficulty: 1

The Need: Do

6 USE A BETTER BROWSER

Internet Explorer is still the most used web browser for regular people, but *Google Chrome* and *Mozilla Firefox* have been the favorite for more advanced computer users for years.

Chrome and *Firefox* are both less likely to be infected by the accidental ad clicks and fake web sites. As well as other built in security features that I won't go into detail about that make them safer.

Both browsers have been considered faster than IE, that's why they first gained popularity.

Adobe's Flash player has been a known security risk for years. Virus or malware makers target *Flash* as their way into your computer. See chapter 21 for more on *Flash*.

Chrome has its own version of *Flash* built in that they keep updated and "sandboxed" from affecting your computer better than *IE* needing to install the *Flash* plugin. In September 2016 *Chrome* is scheduled to not run flash automatically thereby making it even safer.

Firefox still needs *Flash* to be installed but in July of 2015 *Firefox* made it be a "click to run" option so flash won't play automatically, making it safer.

Both browsers allow the installation of small programs called "add-ons" that allow extra functionality. This functionality is also another reason why *Chrome* and *Firefox* are preferred by tech savvy users. These add-ons play a big role in a lot of my security suggestions in the following chapters.

***

Recommendation: Use *Firefox* or *Chrome* as your web browser.

Chrome is more popular and works best with Google services.

Firefox allows one of the more advanced add-ons I will suggest later for people who feel they need the maximum security options.

Chrome – Google.com/chrome/browser

Firefox – Mozilla.org/firefox

The Work: Installing a new web browser if you don't already have one.

Difficulty: 1

The Need: Do

7 USE AN AD BLOCKER

The internet, as we know it, has had advertisements since almost the beginning. At first it was just linked text, and then came banner ads.

Today's web sites have the most annoying ads ever. With ads that open in the middle of the page and make you close them, ones that move across the page, to ones that can take over the whole page that you can't close.

There is not a problem with ads. Web sites need to make money. I have ads on my web sites. I even have used some of the ads on web sites to buy things so they would get the credit. Ads are fine.

I have no problem with reading an article and having to scroll a little more down the page to get past an ad in the middle of the page - as long as it is clear that there is an ad there and not disguised as part of the article. I don't mind watching a few seconds of an ad in a video. As long as it is not longer than the video I plan to watch and I can skip it if it is too long and not of interest to me.

The problem with the ads today is that many of the ads are created by or are infected by bad people trying to spread their malware or a virus.

In fact most studies show ads don't work all that well on the internet. We have become used to ignoring the banner ads. That's why we have todays annoying ads. That's why google and amazon want to "track" your internet usage so they can show you ads that would be of interest to you. Too bad they are not very good at it yet.

There is no getting rid of ads on the internet unless every site becomes a pay per view site. So there is an ad revolution coming. By this I mean more and more people are using ad blockers, so more web sites are detecting this and prompting you with a message about disabling the ad blocker. And advertising companies are looking for new ways to display ads that can't be blocked (and that's ok because this should prevent the virus and malware issue also).

A few (not many yet) web sites are even going so far as to block you, if you have an ad blocker.

An ad blocker is exactly what the name suggests. It is a small program (or extension) that will block ads on web sites.

Ad blockers can do much more than just block ads.

The ad blocking is kind of a side effect of what the programs actually do.

These ad blockers actually block what makes tracking you, and installing stuff, and displaying content pulled from the internet other than the page you're visiting.

So this blocks flash, java, some java script, tracking, and installs. And that is how ads are put on a web page.

The good thing about the ad blockers is that you can turn them off on sites you want or need to support with ads, or if a site won't work with the ad blocker on.

For instance, when I first started using an ad blocker, weather.com would not work. Much of how it displayed the maps used the features that where blocked. Unfortunately, at the time weather.com was a source of some questionable advertisements that I tracked down to be the source of some customer's installation of unwanted fake or misleading antivirus programs. The ad blocker I used, had different settings that could be adjusted to make the page work, but I feel that is too much for the average person do mess with. Today ad blockers have learned how to work on that and other pages (or the sites have changed the way they display their content) so ad blockers – especially the ones I will recommend work on weather.com and most every major site with few issues.

To add (install) the ad blockers, you need to install a small program designed to add features to your web browser called "extensions" or "add-ons". The 3 main browsers people are familiar with *Internet Explorer*, *Google Chrome*, and *Mozilla Firefox* all support extensions. Microsoft's new browser in Windows 10 called *Edge* is supposed to start supporting extensions in early 2016. It is even supposed to support extensions designed for *Chrome*. I hate to say that I am not using *Edge* because it does not support them yet. Other than the lack of extensions, I like *Edge*. It seems much faster than IE.

Each browser has a section in its settings for extensions or add-ons. I will walk you through the process of adding these to your browser.

Chrome:
Click on the menu icon in the upper right corner. Then "settings". Then "extensions" on the left menu. Now you see a list of what extensions you have. At the bottom, you see a link that says "get more extensions". Click on it.

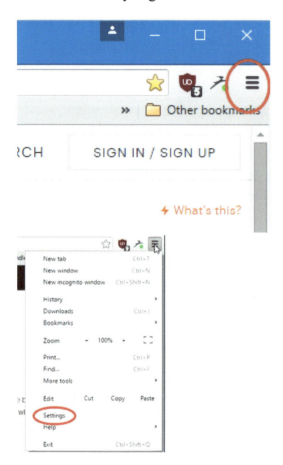

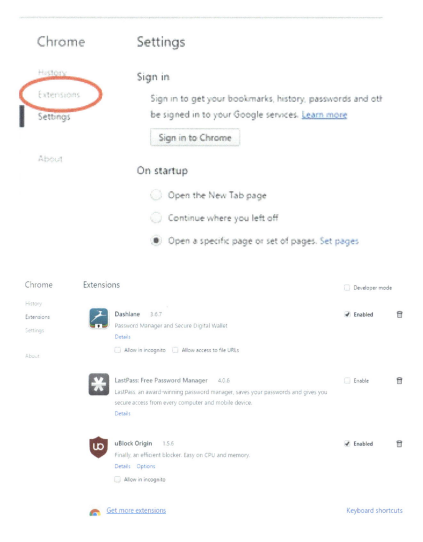

Now you are at the Chrome web store, and can get extensions, themes, and full programs Google offers. Your curser should be in the search box in the upper left side of the screen. Now type in the name of what you are looking for. (see below)

At the top of the results page, you will see Apps, look down a little for the Extensions. On the right of the image / name, you will see a "+ Add to Chrome" button. Add the one you want. Follow its setup instructions.

Firefox:

Click on the menu icon in the upper right corner. Then "Add-ons". You're now at the Add-on store and can do a search from the upper right corner. Now look through the results list for the Add-on you want (see below) and click the install button to the right of its icon / name. Follow its setup instructions.

You can also click on "Extensions" on the left hand menu to see what extensions you have installed. Here you could enable or disable them.

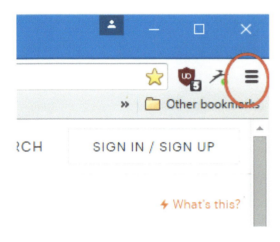

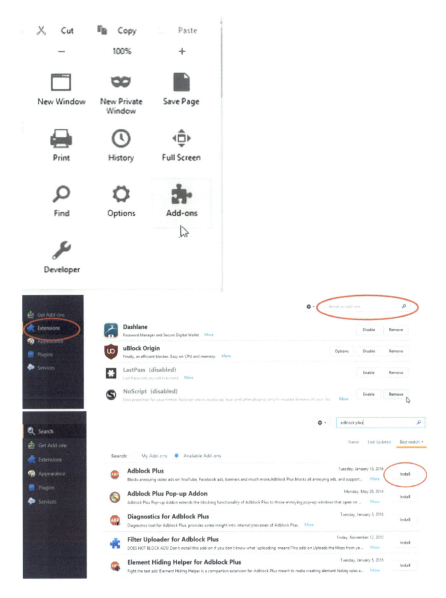

Internet explorer:

Click on the settings icon in the upper right corner. (it looks like a gear sprocket) Then "Manage Add-ons". You're now at the Manage Add-ons window looking at your current toolbars and extensions. Near the bottom, there is a link to

"Find more toolbars and extensions". Click on it and you will be taken to Microsoft's "Internet explorer Gallery" There is a limited number of add-ons from the gallery. Most IE add-ons are downloaded from the internet directly. Luckily the one went is listed in the gallery. Now look through the results list for *Adblock Plus* and click the "add" button to the right of its icon / name. Follow its setup instructions. At time of publishing, you are prompted to save the file and then click the downloaded file at the bottom of the browser to install it.

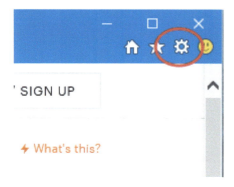

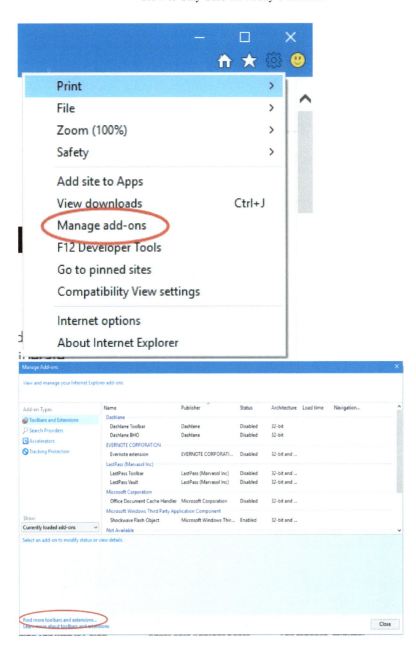

Microsoft Edge:

At the time of publication, *Edge* did not offer extensions, they are scheduled to add extensions early to mid 2016. The process should be very similar to *Internet Explorer's*.

Many extensions can be found by searching the web and going directly to the publisher's web site and clicking on install. But since there can be so many fake sites, I recommend getting them directly from the browsers store unless you know exactly what you're doing.

There are currently 2 Ad blocking extensions I recommend; uBlock Origin, and Adblock Plus. There are many more out there if you find out about another one and want to try it. Just make sure you trust the source like Cnet.com, PC Magazine, or other reputable tech web site (Such as my technology news blog Techbreakdown.tv).

Recommendation: uBlock Origin for Chrome and Firefox.

Internet Explorer: Adblock Plus

> (At the time of publication, uBlock Origin was not available for IE)

Adblock Plus was the original ad blocker and still works fine. But through the years it has gotten reviews and test results that indicate it is slowing down Firefox and Chrome. There are also some concerns about how they are now allowing some ads through for money.

uBlock Origin seems to be faster and works fine with no customization.

Using the uBlock Origin:

Once uBlock Origin is installed you will see its icon near the top of your browser window after the address bar. It is a red shield with UO (looks like UD to me) and a small number in black. That number is the number of things it is blocking. How many do you see on the sites you visit????

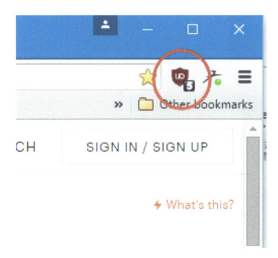

If you click the icon, you get a little window open under the icon. At the top of that window, there is a big universal power button icon. It is a circle with a line going half way through at the top - (if you look at your computer, tablet, or other electronics you should see it on or near their power buttons). It should be blue. If you click on that big power button icon, it will turn grey and stop blocking things on that site. So if you visit a site that does not work, or asks you to turn off your ad blocker, you can turn it off.

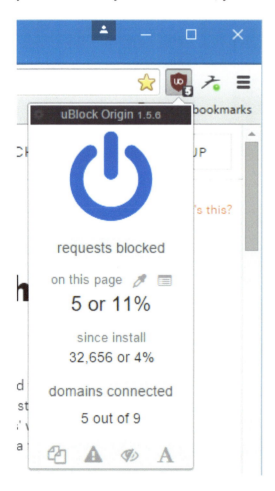

You many need to refresh the site to see the new look.

The icon at the top also turns grey so you know that site is not being blocked.

Of course, turning blocking back on is done the same way. Click on the big grey power icon.

The little window for uBlock Origin also shows you other information like how many other web sites the site you are on is connecting to for ads or other information.

There are also more advanced controls at the bottom bar of the window. You can experiment with these if you like or visit their site for detailed instructions, but for most users just turning uBlock Origin on and off is all you need to do.

Using Adblock Plus:

Once Adblock Plus is installed you will see its icon near the top of your browser window after the address bar. It is a red "stop sign" like shield with the letters ABP.

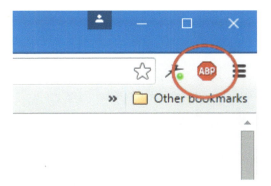

Like uBlock Origin, if you click on the icon you will get a menu. The top line of the menu says weather ABP is enabled or disabled on the site. Clicking on that line will change if ads are blocked or not.

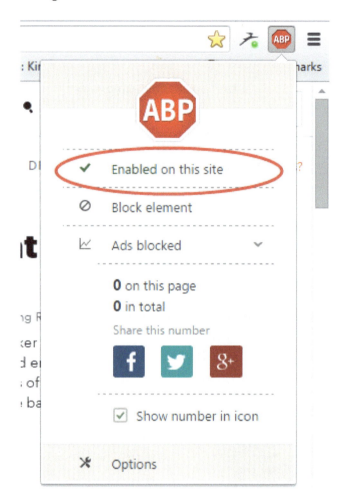

On the bottom of the menu you can choose "options" for more advanced settings. You can experiment with these if you like or visit their site for detailed instructions, but for most users just turning Adblock Plus on and off is all you need to do.

* At the time of writing this book, Ablock Plus would not install on IE 11 on Windows 10.   ***

***

Recommendation: Install an ad blocker. *uBlock Origin

The Work: Install ad blocker extensions / add-ons.

Difficulty: 1

The Need: Do

8 USE STONG PASSWORDS!

I know passwords are a pain in the ass.

But, you NEED TO HAVE LONG, RANDOM, and STRONG PASSWORDS.

You also NEED TO STOP USING THE SAME PASSWORD ON ALL SITES!

Believe me; I know it a pain in the ass!

The next chapter will talk about using password managers. Password managers are an easy way to make and keep track of very strong and different passwords for every site.

This (password issues) is the reason I started writing this book. It grew from a pamphlet I was going to give to customers to a book.

I will show you how to have great, even awesome passwords in a way that you can use them. You may even feel some pride when you tell people while talking; that you honestly could not tell them your Facebook password.

Everyone "knows" they should have a good password, but good passwords are hard to remember. So, you use the same password for multiple sites; maybe with some variation or numbers. Remember in the introduction; I mentioned that security is not easy.

If you do use the same or very similar passwords for multiple sites it makes it easy for someone to log into other accounts if one of them is hacked or stolen. i.e. News reports of Yahoo.com passwords being hacked. If someone gets your Yahoo password, they then try that email and password on other big sites like amazon or banking sites.

Also using the name of someone or a pet is easy for people who know you or looks at your Facebook page to guess.

An example: jenny123 = bad password.

Some people write down their passwords in a booklet and keep it at their computer desk. This is not a good idea because if someone breaks into your house they will look for things like this. It can also be hard to use sometimes, especially if you need a password when you're not at home or forget to update it. You may not know it, but you could have passwords for close to 100 web sites. 20-30 is completely common.

Don't save your passwords in a note or word document called "passwords" on your computer.

If someone would hack your computer or even sit down at your computer they could find that in 10 seconds.

You can save your passwords on your computer ***if you can password protect it*** like in Micorosoft's *OneNote* program. When you put a password on a *OneNote* document it gets encrypted. If you are an apple user, you can password protect your *Pages* or *Numbers* documents, they also get encrypted when there is a password.

You can use this as a way to have a backup method to look up your passwords. Just in case there is an issue with getting to your password manager from the next chapter.

What is a strong password?

From Webopedia.com: "A **strong password** consists of at least six characters (and the more characters, the stronger the password) that are a combination of letters, numbers, and symbols (@, #, $, %, etc.) if allowed. Passwords are typically case-sensitive, so a **strong password** contains letters in both uppercase and lowercase."

Their definition needs updated to make the number at least 8 instead of 6, but I took it for the explanation.

Actually I recommend at least 10 characters for any password.

For sites that are more important like online banking, credit cards, and shopping such as Amazon go 20 characters. You can vary the number from 18-25 or more – if the site allows. Some sites have a limit smaller than 20. For them use the max number or close to it. Theoretically, if you use the max number of say 8, someone trying to hack the site could limit their tries to passwords with just 8 characters. This could take as little as 1 day. Password strength depends on the attacker not knowing how long it is. A hacker has to try every password from 1 character to the max.

"20 characters?! I'll never remember that, that's crazy", You say?

Remember; **you won't need to remember the password**. You will use a password manger to do this for you.

The website you are on should have some text near the password field letting you know what you can put in as far as number of characters and what symbols can be used. You may need to click on an ? icon near the password field if it is not plainly visible.

Password strength:

Use at least 8 characters. Don't use a password from another site, or something too obvious like your pet's name. Why?

Create a password

You can't leave this empty.

Confirm your password

Length is the key to password security. A password that is 1 character longer than another takes 95 times longer to hack. It doesn't seem like 1 character would make sooo much difference huh? But it does. So having a password around 20 characters long is essentially impossible to be hacked.

Some security experts say, if length is key, then you can have a password that looks fairly simple as long as it has letters (upper and lower case), numbers, and symbols.

Example from GRC.com
: D0g…………….   0 is a zero.
is stronger than JdXhs.N(n5k87@M&

The second example is 16 characters, random, and has all the needed characters. It is a very good password. It would take 1.41 hundred million centuries to crack! Not bad huh. But the first one using dog as a base and adding a capital letter, 0, and 17 special characters making it 20 digits long is 11.52 thousand trillion centuries! to crack.

Either one is essentially un-crackable. But for security sake why not make it as hard as possible.

You don't want to use 17 periods, that is just an example for length.

So you can have a password that is easy to look at and possibly remember but be completely safe. You can try to use 3 – 4 words. If you use capital letters, small letters, numbers, and special characters mixed in.

So if you wanted to, you could create a password like:
    jennY@likeS!dogS^23$
With capital letters mixed in, special characters between the words and one at the end, and a couple numbers.

This still is not easy to remember with the special characters, but it would give you a base to at least think it is easy to remember.

Of course, you don't want to use the same words and special characters on multiple sites. So don't use "jenny likes dogs" or @!^$ as the base on another site.

Having at least 20 sites to have good passwords still means

you won't be able to remember your password.

You will need and should use a password manager. See next chapter.

I still use the full completely random passwords; partially because my password manager creates them for me. Also because you really can't remember these passwords, it does not matter if it looks easy or not.

Even though I gave examples of passwords taking 11.52 thousand trillion centuries to crack or the one that takes about a day, you won't need to worry about that. Most web sites have a limited number of tries before the account gets locked. Most banking or shopping sites limit is 3-5 attempts. That is the main reason having a 20 digit password is essentially impossible to crack. The 11.52 thousand trillion centuries to crack is for when the database gets stolen and a hacker has direct access to it – not through the internet. That is also why you would still change your password if a website says THEY were hacked.

*Top Secret - Only in This Book! – tip *

Create long complicated <u>user names</u> the same way you would passwords when possible.

You may think that your email is a required user name for most sites. Well many sites let you create a unique user name not related to email. So you can create a user name like D%li3si#kk(IS*4. This keeps people from even trying to log on to a site if your email address gets stolen or is tried randomly. (You may not be able to use special characters. So you can keep it to just words and numbers.)

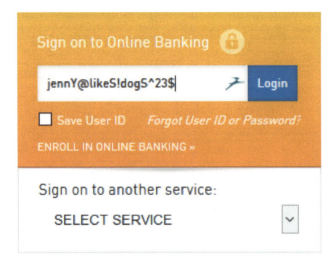

Other tips:

Don't just use the words of your email address without the @.com or a common name.

Don't use your first and last name as a user name or an email address.

You don't want to give anyone online any personal information you don't have to and your name is very powerful to hackers and identity thieves. You don't want to make the user name something easy for someone who knows you to try.

I came across this idea when one of my credit card web sites kept telling me that my account was locked because of too many failed attempts to log on. At first I thought it was me, I changed my password and moved on. Then I got that message 3 months in a row. So it dawned on me that someone had figured out my user name for the site and kept trying to log in. – At the time the user name was the same as my email address without the @.com. So someone got my email address (maybe knew it was associated to the credit card or maybe just random). So it was a good thing that I had a strong password!

Trying to prevent this from happening again, I realized I could use anything for a user name. So I made up some long complicated user name (with the 3 word system) just like I would a password. I have not had that problem again, and I have extended it to my most important sites.

This is something I have not heard ANY OTHER security expert or source suggest. I think it can be a key to keeping accounts from being attacked.

* If you hear a site has been hacked, you would still want to change your user name and / or password.

If you are informed that a site has had a security issue and are told to change your password, remember DON'T CLICK ON A LINK FROM AN EMAIL to change it. Visit the site from your bookmarks or by typing it in. Hopefully no main site will send you an email with a link in it these days. (see Chapter 19)

***

Recommendation: Use long complicated passwords *and* user names.

The Work: Think of or use a password manager to create strong
passwords.

Difficulty: 1

The Need: Do

9 USE A PASSWORD MANAGER

As stated in the last chapter you need to have a strong, long, complicated password these days. Passwords that you **can not** remember and you should not write down for people to find. Passwords that are a pain in the ass.

This means you need what's called a password manager.

As you can figure out, this is a program that will keep all of your passwords. They can usually keep other information too. You can store credit card numbers and other notes.

The password manager can also generate strong passwords for you as you join a new site.

There are many options out there. All of the main antivirus programs offer a password management feature now. Web browsers will offer to keep your passwords too. I recommend separate programs from companies that specialize in passwords.

Your web browser also offers to remember passwords for you. Its easy, but there are usually concerns that if the browser gets infected with malware or virus, they could gain access to that information and they do not generate passwords for you.

Antivirus company password managers: these are usually toolbars or a separate program from the antivirus company itself. So you could use Norton's password Manager even if you don't use their antivirus. ~~If you already use one of these or feel more comfortable with one because the name recognition that is fine.~~

*While writing this book, there where multiple news reports on how password managers or web browsers from antivirus companies had VERY BAD security flaws. I will NOT RECOMMEND using any program from an antivirus company that is not their main antivirus program!

You want to use a Password Manager program: There are many programs that specialize in password management. I can't even name them all, but I will mention / cover the ones I am familiar with or know are safe and reputable.

There is LastPass, Dashlane, KeyPass, Roboform, and 1Password. All work on Windows, Mac, phones, and tablets.

LastPass is widely considered one of, if not the best, password manager. It has been examined and backed by security expert Steve Gibson. It is the password manager I use. It is free, but you get more features like syncing with multi devices like PCs, phones, Tablets, advanced multi factor authentication for only $12 a year. I think your internet security is worth $1 a month. You will need LastPass to be on your phone or tablet as well as your PC for quick access and regular 2 factor authentication.

Dashlane is a newer player but has gained a lot of traction in the past few years. It has a $30 yearly fee for syncing between devices. I paid and used it for a year (alongside LastPass). It is the best looking program with large icons and a slick interface. I liked it fine, but found LastPass to be easier to use on an Android phone. If you like this one, $30 or maybe less on sale is also a good price for security. (While writing this book, LastPass updated their interface to be similar to Dashlane's so it looks nicer now too.)

Key Pass is one of the original password managers and was one of the first to offer security features like using a USB drive. But it still has a very old interface and is for advanced users.

Roboform offers a toolbar in your web browser and was also an early contender.... It is also pretty basic in its interface but I have seen some regular people use it just fine.

1Password was originally for Mac only, but now works on Windows and your phone. There is a yearly cost of $50. But it is generally considered the best password manager by die hard Apple users.

All of the password managers have a tutorial when you install it and a how-to on their web site or app. They are mostly self-explanatory and easy to learn. They know you are not a computer expert.

***

Recommendation: Use 1. LastPass. 2. Dashlane or
3. 1 Password.

The Work: Install the password manager on PC and other devices. Spend some time learning how to use it.

Difficulty: 2

The Need: Do

10 DON'T ANSWER SECURITY QUESTIONS TRUTHFULLY

You know those "secret questions" most web sites ask you as a security check if you try to reset your password?

Never put in the true answer to those questions. If someone knows you or nowadays if someone can search your social media accounts they can get answers to most of those questions.

In the early days of the internet those questions where a good idea. But even then they were simple questions that if people knew you they might be able to answer. To their credit sites are getting more creative with those questions so it is not so easy.

Something I have done and suggested to people for 10 years (and an idea that is gaining popularity in the security community) is to answer those questions with completely non related words or even a password like response and save them in your password manager. The password managers in the last chapter will let you save notes along with the password.

For example: the common question of "what is your mother's maiden name?" can be answered with "dog food" or "h65jsirthg7".

A possible trick to use to make it easier would be to pick a word or phrase and add a number to it for each new question and site.

For example: dog food 1, dog food 2, and dog food 3 can be the answer to one sites questions and dog food 4, 5, and 6 can be the next web sites answers. And so on..

When you need to answer the question, just look it up in your password manager.

No one will be able to guess, look up, or get lucky and answer those questions, making it much harder for someone to take over your account.

***

Recommendation: Answer secret questions websites use as a security check with random words or a password like response and save them in your password manager.

The Work: create and save unique answers to security questions.

Difficulty: 1

The Need: Should Do

11 USE 2-FACTOR AUTHENTICATION

This chapter is one of the harder security measures to take because you need to make sure you keep web sites up to date with phone numbers or email addresses or you need to remember to use another app on your phone.

You may have seen this term on some sites like Google or your bank asking you to set up *two factor* or *multi factor authentication.* And you have probably ignored it or did not want to be bothered with checking it out. Some may have tried to set it up but got nervous about doing it.

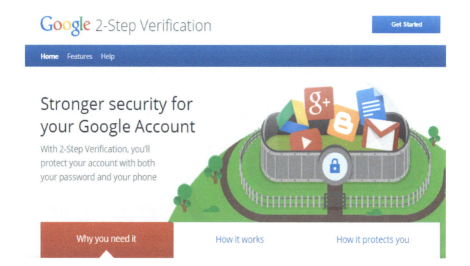

Two factor authentication is simply letting the site use a second way to confirm you are you after you enter your password. It is like places asking for 2 forms of ID when you fill out credit applications or other legal forms.

This two factor authentication is usually only needed the first time you log on to that site from a specific computer or device. Like many things, it will remember you after that. So if someone got your password and tried to log on from a computer in NY and you live in Arizona, they would be prompted for this code and not be able to get in.

Today that second form of authentication is most commonly your cell phone number so the website can send you a text message with a code or pin number to enter into the site. You can usually also give them a different email address than the one you signed up with. Just make sure you can check that email address in the future. (see chapter 18) I have had customers get prompted for an email address they say they have not used for years and don't remember its password. If you can't access that second email, your out of luck.

A text message as 2-factor authentication.

The idea is, if you can access a second thing they know should belong to you; your you. Using a cell phone is best for a couple of reasons. First and from a security view point, only you should be able to receive a text sent to your phone. So if a hacker in Russia is trying to break into your bank account, they won't have your cell phone. Second for a personal convenience point, most people have their cell phone on them all the time. So you can get the text even if you're not home.

You then need to make sure you update sites with your phone number if you ever change it. Just like people not being able to access an old email, if you can't get the text message. You're out of luck.

Of course it is good to give them a second email and phone number because you may not have access to one of them but can access the other.

Another way of two factor authentication is using an app on your phone from Google (called Google Authenticator) or Facebook (built into the Facebook app). A website can ask you for a code that these apps generate. This way you don't need to wait for an email or text or worry about the site having a wrong phone number or email address.

Sometimes you could set the sites to ask for that authentication each time you log on. This can be very annoying so most people don't set this up. If you have a reason like identity theft victims or something else, it can be done.

*** *

Recommendation: Set up two factor authentication; at least for important sites like banking, credit cards, email, and Amazon.

The Work: Keeping all of your sites up to date with phone and email, setting up the authentication.

Difficulty: 3 – because of work needed to keep sites updated or use the app.

The Need: Should Do

For an even more advanced form of authentication, you can search for "multi factor authentication USB" in your favorite search engine.

12 DON'T CLICK ON THAT FIRST SEARCH RESULT

The title of this chapter pretty much says it all. Unfortunately the first couple results when you do a web search are usually advertisements.

As I have said before, there is nothing wrong with advertisements, but these ads are often put there by the bad guys. You click on the first result that looks good, and you are taken to a bad site that directly installs a virus or is full of other links that will. Possibly have fake "update your flash player" messages I talk about in the next chapter.

See the line separating the ads from the search results?

You can tell the first few results are ads because there is some kind of distinction in the background color or even a line or box separating them from the rest of the normal results.

So you need to look at the search page carefully to see if the first ones look like ads or not.

Of course you should look at any search result closely before clicking on it. The bad guys are good at making their pages show up on top of any search.

Under the search result title, you can see the actual web page it leads to. Look at that line and see if it looks.... weird. If you don't like where it's going to take you, don't click on it.

For example: if you search for "Norton virus removal" you may get...

Norton 360 – Spyware Removal | Norton Store
buy.**norton**.com/en-us/**norton**-360/MggKOTIxNzY0Chl0cm9ubm90... ˅
Norton 360 offers advanced protection for your PC with features such as **anti virus** and **spyware** removal. Buy **Norton** 360 Software from the official **Norton** Store by ...

Norton Products by Symantec
www.symantec-**norton**.com/**Norton_AntiVirus**_Free_30-Day... ˅
Norton Discount and Download Center for the US - Buy, Upgrade or Renew **Norton** Products. Quick, Easy and Secure! → NEW SPECIAL OFFERS WON'T LAST!

The first link will take you to Norton.com and is safe. The second one will take you to "Symantec-norton.com"; It looks like it goes to Norton, but does not. This is very questionable and I would not click on that link.

Sometimes these sites have weird names like **security2k.net** – does that look like a normal website you've ever visited before? NO. So Don't visit it.

                                    ***

Recommendation: look at your search results for being ads and where they actually go.

The Work: Being observant.

Difficultly: 1

The Need: Do

13 PAY ATTENTION TO POP UPS / BEWARE FAKE UPDATES

One of the biggest ways people get toolbars and other unwanted programs on their computer or don't keep their computer updated is that they don't pay attention to pop up windows. Either they just say "ok" to a message and get tricked into installing something – and get something they did not want installed, or close the pop up – and don't get an updated installed.

Yes those pop ups can be annoying, and they seem to come at the worst time. But, you need to pay attention to those pop ups and read them. It just takes a few seconds. Then you can decide what to do. DON'T JUST SAY "OK".

If the pop up sounds like it wants to install something think; "did I do something to start that?" or "Did I mean to install that?" if the answer is NO, then say NO to the pop up. If you are not sure, say NO. If it is something important it will come up again.

Example: You visit a site to play a game or watch a video. On the top of the page, on what looks like a video window is a message saying "You need to update your Flash Player to watch this video". You think "OK, usually the video shows up. If it is not showing up I must need an update"....

But you don't need an update, you just visited a bad web site that is designed just to get you to click on that link and install a virus or malware.

Almost never will you get a legitimate message to update Flash when you try to watch a video.

Never install something from a web site or pop ups from a web page.

Clicking on links to go to a web page or search result should not start an install. You should want to install something like a new web browser to get that kind of pop up.

If you did not go looking for it, don't install it.

If the pop up wants to update something like Flash look at it close and think "did that come up after I got to a web page or clicked on a video?" or did it come up shortly after the computer turned on?

FAKE

This fake one is trying to tell you that you need a new flash to view the site.

 REAL

This real update comes on your desktop, usually shortly after the computer starts up.

If a message to update Adobe comes up on your **desktop** shortly after your computer turned on then it should be the real thing. Adobe updates should not be triggered by visiting a web page or clicking on a video!

Windows and Java updates show up in the lower right corner of your desktop. Never from web pages either. Windows should just update on its own if you set up auto updates from chapter 5. It will prompt you and you can choose to install them manually or just wait till you reboot your computer.

Phone Tip:
Cell phones get pop up ads too!

Some web sites will show them but since most people use free apps, they have ads in them.

Don't believe any ad or pop up on a cell phone telling you IT is infected!

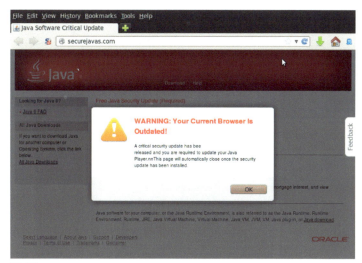

FAKE

This pop-up is from a web site and saying you need an update to use their page.

REAL

Another scam that seemed to explode in 2015 was the fake phone support ads that took over your web page or desktop. These fake ads showed a message indicating you had virus infections and you should call a phone number for help. When you called this number, you would usually be charged $200 - $300. This call would remove the full screen ad and install some other antivirus program on your computer for 1 year of "support". The problem was, all the person needed to do was restart the computer to remove the ad. And the program that was installed slowed down the computer and could even let more damaging infections on the computer.

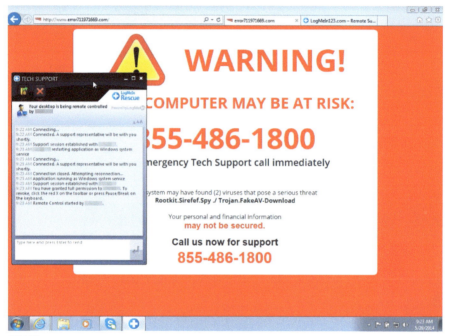

FAKE

Never call a support phone number that you see on the internet, a pop up window or program window!

NO LEGITIMATE COMPANY INCLUDING NORTON AND MICROSOFT WILL ASK YOU TO CALL THEM! – Even if you have Norton antivirus.

Tip:

A variant of this is that you **get a phone call** from someone claiming to be from Norton, Microsoft, or your internet company offering to clean your computer because they see it is infected. They proceed to show you error messages that "prove" you are infected. Then they install some other antivirus program on your computer. But these "error messages" are normal errors that happen to every computer every day and don't cause any real problem. Now you have a fake antivirus or tune up program on your computer causing real issues and out $200 - $300.

Once these people are on your computer, there is no telling what they can do. They can infect you with real virus's download files or information to steal your identity. They can even run up your credit card once they have it.

Tell them you don't even have a computer, and if you are worried take it to a local technician.

NO LEGITIMATE COMPANY INCLUDING NORTON AND MICROSOFT WILL CALL YOU!

***

Recommendation: Take a moment to look at pop up messages and determine if it is something you meant to do or should say NO to it.

The Work: Be observant of pop ups and update messages

Difficulty: 1

The Need: Do

14 DON'T DOWNLOAD TOOLBARS

Another big annoyance is having a lot of tool bars across the top of your web browser. Especially to those of us who work on computers. When a customer brings in a PC with a lot of toolbars, we just cringe. I have seen as many as 20 toolbars on someone's computer. So much that you can only use half the screen. I think 3 is a common amount people get.

Too many toolbars!

Most people even say "I don't know how those got there".

Those toolbars get there when you visit a page and there is a little pop up that says something like "help improve your search" and you click on it; maybe just to get rid of the message and it installs a toolbar. Even Yahoo, Microsoft, and Google are guilty of this.

You can also get them when you download something like the Google Chrome browser or a game. (See Chapter 15 for extra programs getting installed)

One of the worst is the toolbar from Ask.com. It gets on your computer when you visit one of their sites from a web search or download. Ask.com was once a good search engine, but now is known for its ads and annoying toolbar. This toolbar is one that does not always uninstall either.

The ones from Yahoo, Microsoft, and Google are …. Ok. Especially if you use their services a lot and actually will use that toolbar. But usually you can just search from the address bar just fine. I don't recommend having a tool bar even from them unless you really use it.

The problem comes when you end up with multiple tool bars. Especially if they come from someplace that tries to take over your search – and injects fake advertising to your web sites. This is when a toolbar become malware.

Also, these toolbars can create security holes in your web browser that can allow virus & malware in. Possibly worse yet, well more annoying anyway, is these toolbars from bad sites are not written (programed) well and can cause your browser to crash. And crash, and crash.

Whenever someone would say they were having trouble surfing the internet / have crashes, and we see more than 1 toolbar (especially 10+), we knew right away what the main problem was.

I would suggest if you have a lot of toolbars, especially more than 3, you take your computer to a local technician. Because if you have that many toolbars, odds are very good you have some kind of virus / malware also.

If you want to remove just one or 2, hopefully you can do that just by clicking on the small x that is usually on the top right or left corner of that toolbar. Say "yes" to the prompt that asks "are you sure you want to remove this toolbar". But if the toolbar is from a bad source, that x may not work.

You can also turn off or remove toolbars from the same settings screen as *extensions* from chapter 7 where controlled.

Chrome:
Click on the menu icon in the upper right corner. Then "settings". Then "extensions" on the left menu. Now you see a list of what extensions you have. Find the one you want to remove and either "disable" or "remove".

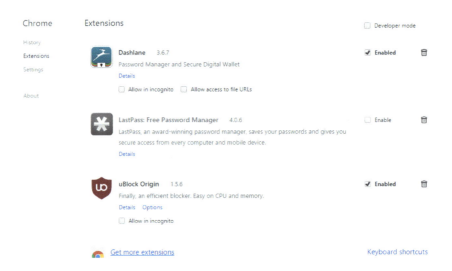

Firefox:
Click on the menu icon in the upper right corner. Then "Add-ons". You can highlight the toolbar you wish to remove. At the bottom right of the full window, you should see an option to "disable" or possibly "remove". Chose one of those options.

Internet explorer:

Click on the settings icon in the upper right corner. (it looks like a gear sprocket) Then "Manage Add-ons". Here you will see the "Toolbars and extensions" window. You can highlight the toolbar you wish to remove. At the bottom right of the full window, you should see an option to "disable" or possibly "remove". Chose one of those options.

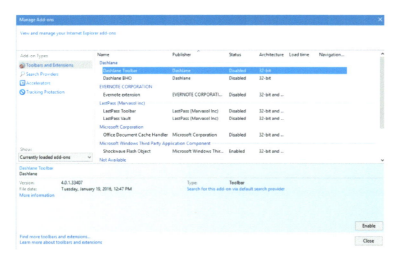

If you have trouble removing those pesky toolbars, or the computer does not run well afterwards see a local technician.

∗∗∗

Recommendation: When asked to install a toolbar from any site (Even Yahoo, Microsoft, and Google) say "No".

The Work: Don't install toolbars if you see a prompt for one.

Difficulty: 1

The Need: Do

15 BEWARE EXTRA SOFTWARE INSTALLS

When you do install or even update some software, you need to be careful about the company installing other software too.

Since a lot of what people install themselves is free from the internet, that company tries to make money by including other software in the download. This other software will install and run in the background slowing down your computer. Often they will install 2 or 3 programs you did not know would install. These are often fake tune up or fake antivirus programs that you can't close and slow down your computer when they run. That makes them malware.

These programs can just be annoying by slowing down your computer or popping up and making you close them. But they may be more dangerous. If they are fake antivirus programs they often ask for money. They may also be a link to other more dangerous virus or malware, and pretty soon you are fully infected and can't use your computer.

This has become a very common practice today. Even the once trusted Download.com (part of cnet.com) has started including these extra programs. I no longer use or suggest them for safe downloads anymore.

One big example of this is (guess who) *Adobe Flash* install or update usually wants to install a McAfee antivirus scanner(sometimes another program). It will do this even if you have an antivirus program installed.

You need to make sure that the check box allowing this install is NOT
CHECKED.

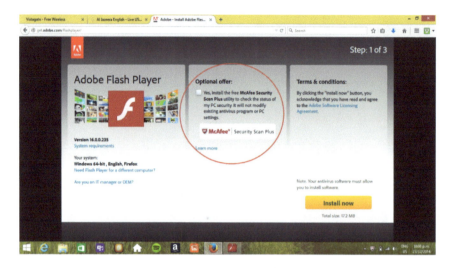

This from adobe is not really dangerous. It is more annoying. They will
prompt you to buy McAfee antivirus. Sometimes people forget they
already have something installed and they buy McAfee too. So they
have bought 2 antivirus programs.

**When a program first starts to install you can usually see a check box
or a link saying that this extra software will be installed. Sometimes
you even have to click on a link for "advanced setup" or "custom
setup". Then you will see these check boxes and you can uncheck
them.**

I suggests whenever installing something, especially from the internet,
look for "advanced setup" or "custom setup" instead of using the
"quick" install option. Sometimes this will give you a page or 2 showing
you where the program will be installed and if other programs will be
installed with it. You should be able to choose not to install those other
programs.

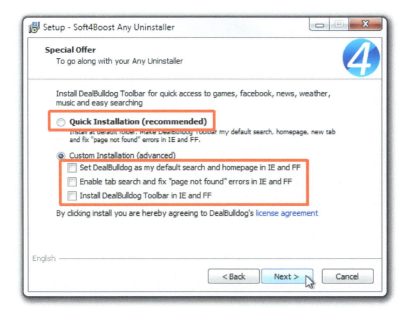

***

Recommendation: Take care when installing or updating software to make sure extra software installs are not included.

The Work: Be observant when installing software, check advanced setup or custom setup options.

Difficulty: 1

The Need: Should Do

16 BACKUP BACKUP

Backing up your files is the most important thing you should do.

Backing up is so important that I am reminding you a couple times throughout this book.

"Punk you better backup" – Cypress Hill, Jump Around.

17 USE WEB MAIL

This suggestion is more for future convenience and to help future technicians who may work on your computer. It is also a pet peeve of mine.

Email programs like outlook, outlook express, or Incredimail are now outdated and a dying race. All email has moved online. The main email providers are online companies. Google, Yahoo, Microsoft, and ISPs have good online interfaces. Work email is the only good reason to use a program now. Work is also the main reason most people use a program at home. We just got used to having it.

The main reason email programs exist is there originally was no other way to get email. When the internet and email first started they just sent information back and forth between servers. There had to be a way for humans to read the email.

Then AOL came and people started getting their email from AOLs web site.

Now, like everything else, email is a web page experience.

Think about how difficult it can be to get your email information into outlook. You have to look up *POP mail servers* and usually call your internet company for help.

Most ISPs don't support those programs anymore. These days your internet companie probably won't help you set up the email program if you call them. They will direct you to a web page with the settings. Other than that you're probably on your own. Why? Because they want you to use the web interface, and they won't need to spend time or money on the phone talking about the old programs.

Switching to the internet version of the email can save you, and any computer tech who may work on your computer, hassle and frustration when you get a new computer or need to have work done that requires the deletion of those email programs.

Unfortunately, moving mail from one computer to another is not as easy as people think (as it should be). Moving the mail often messes up the folder structure. So it's frustrating to people who wanted everything exactly as it was, and to the technician trying to please a customer.

Email programs get discontinued. A lot of people are familiar with Outlook Express from Microsoft. Well, Outlook Express has not been around since 2005! Iit was last included in Windows XP. It has been replaced a couple of times with different programs. Each of these new email programs look a little different, and people don't like trying to learn the new program. Using web based email; you don't need to worry about as much change. Sure companies do change the way their web pages look, but the basic functionality is the same. You just need to take a moment to get used to the new look.

You can access your email from any computer anywhere with the web version and not worry about seeing duplicate emails from one computer to the next.

Using the web based email is also a way to keep email separate. If you have multiple emails (this is a good idea, see next chapter), keeping them in one program can be confusing if you need to keep them separate.

Make Yahoo.com (or MSN...) your home page, if it isn't already. And when you open your web browser, you can see and check your mail right there after looking at the headlines.

If you have an Android phone, it shows you your Gmail automatically.

Tip: Don't use the mail program built into Windows.

My last book, *Windows 8 Sucks, Here's How to Use It*, was partially started because the mail program in Windows 8 was soooooooo bad. Unfortunately, the one in Windows 10 is not much better. At least you can copy and paste text from one email to the other, but if you don't like new things don't try it. Believe me; just start using the web based email.

So next time you think of it, try to start looking at your email on the web. You don't have to go cold turkey. Work your way into it. Hopefully soon, you'll be using the web version and forget about the program and when you get a new computer, that's one less thing you need to worry about setting up.

Move your contacts

You can move or export your contacts to a web mail. Each program may be a little different, but general instructions are:
Click on File, Tools, or Options in the top menu, then look for Export Contacts. Follow the next steps, choosing CSV when prompted to choose what type of file to save. Save it to your desktop. Then in the web email page click the Contacts icon. Look for Tools or Actions, then choose Import Contacts instead of Export. Point the file browser to your desktop and the file you saved there. You may need to do a quick web search for "how to import contacts into..." the mail program you are moving to. (Yahoo, Google, MSN..).

***

Recommendation: Start using web mail, not programs like Outlook Express.

The Work: Switching to web mail. New things are sometimes frustrating.

Difficulty: 2 – just because change is hard.

The Need: Can Do

18 USE MULTIPLE EMAIL ADDRESSES

How many email addresses do you have? Just one? The one from your internet company like Road Runner?

Then you need at least 2 more email addresses. Go to Google, Yahoo or Microsoft and create some more. But you may have more email addresses than you think...

There can be several issues with having just one email address. First if you just have the email from your internet company like Road Runner and you ever move and get a new internet provider you will have to change your email address. You will have to tell all your contacts and update all your web sites. That's a pain!

Second, if someone hacks your 1 email, they can have access to all the information in it and use it to reset passwords for other sites.

Third, you get all that spam mail.

I have at least 10 email addresses. Now you don't need to go that crazy. I don't even check most of them on a regular basis. I have had one of my first email addresses from Yahoo for…. 20 years! But you want to have a couple emails to give for certain situations.

You should have 1 or 2 main email addresses, not from your internet

provider, to give to people and to use for big sites like banking, credit cards, and common shopping sites. This way you never need to change them.

You should have 1or 2 less important emails for less important sites like places you shop once a year, dating sites, or other weird things you need to sign up for but don't want to give them a real email because you know it will just be spam.

One of those email accounts you create you should use for sites you don't plan on ever using again or signing up for coupons or other things you know are going to generate only junk mail. P.s. that's about all you get from coupon and sweepstakes sign ups. They sell your information and you start getting more junk mail – that can have virus links in it.

You may have more email accounts than you think.

Do you have an Android phone? If so then you have a Gmail email address.

Do you have some kind of account with Microsoft for Xbox, Office, or even a Windows Phone? If so then you have an email account with them too. These include Hotmail.com, Outlook.com, and Live.com.

If you have one of these accounts, check into them to make sure you can access it and start using it for one of those purposes.

What to do.

If you need to create new email addresses for one or more of these reasons it's easy. Just go to one (or more) of the providers (Google, Yahoo or Microsoft) and sign up for a new account. They are all free. Google and Microsoft offer many other features like online storage for photos, music, or any data. They both also offer online music and videos. Both of them have very good spam filtering.

Have important web sites send mail to Google, Yahoo or Microsoft so you don't need to change it if you ever move.

Unfortunately then comes the work of creating the accounts and changing at least some of your current web site accounts to the new email addresses. Luckily you don't have to do it all at one time. Maybe change the big ones; you know banking, credit cards, and Amazon. Then change some of the others as you visit them.

This is also a good time to change the password on those sites using your password manager!

I'm not saying don't use your internet provider email at all. Just start using other mails for some things now so it won't be so hard in the future.

***

Recommendation: Have multiple email addresses for junk mail and less important sites, and use Google, Yahoo or Microsoft as your main mail for friends and important sites so you don't have to change them if you move.

The Work: Creating the new accounts, and updating current sites with a new email.

Difficulty: 2 – because of time and effort to create and change info.

The Need: Should Do

19 DON'T CLICK ON LINKS IN EMAIL

This is another one where the title is self-explanatory, and hopefully everyone has heard and "knows" already. Through the history of people getting viruses, the number one way to get infected or get tricked into giving someone else your personal information is to click on a link in an email. Whether it is a word document attached to an email or something that looks like it's from your bank, do not click.

Don't click on links in emails unless you know exactly what it is!

Banks will not (should not) send you an email with links to log in to their site!

Banks will not send you an email with links to reset or confirm your password - or any other info!

NO!

These kind of fake bank emails is called *Phishing*. Because the bad guys are "fishing" for information.

If banks have a security issue, they will inform you there is an issue, and ask you to visit their site the way you normally do to log in or change information, not with a link.

Why is this a problem? Because the link you look at can go to a different site than it shows in words. A link that says bankofamerica.com can go to   GetWorstVirusEver.com (I don't know if that is a real address or not. It's just an example – don't try it) and you are infected.

Word documents will be an attachment and will be saved to your computer, not a link to a web site.
If you were not expecting a Word document from someone, ask them about it before opening.
Your computer and antivirus should both scan this document when it is downloaded and warn you if there is a problem.

In 2015 a major new virus started to gain popularity. Something called *Cryptolocker*. Cryptolocker is a type of *ransomware*. These programs encrypt or scramble your personal data, and it cannot be fixed unless you pay them several hundred dollars. Cryptolocker got on most people's computes by email links.

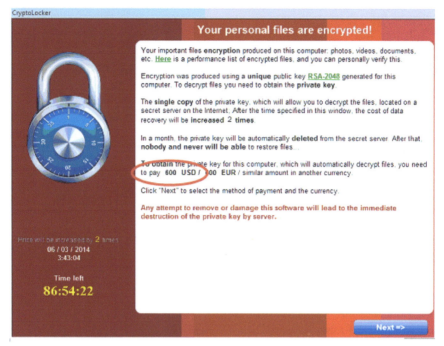

Cryptolocker message.

You may even have heard something about this in the news because many police departments, hospitals, and other high profile places actually had to pay them, because they needed the information so bad.

This type of virus is only going to get more popular because there is no fix. I hated telling customers that there data was gone unless they paid these crooks. Then the only way to really clean the computer is to erase everything and reinstall Windows and all your programs.

What made it harder yet was you often have to pay them in Bitcoins. Bitcoins are something else you have probably heard of in the news or TV shows because it also got popular for a while in 2014. The problem is it's very difficult for the average person to get Bitcoins.

This is also a good reason to back up your data so see chapter 1 and its special tip.

***

Recommendation: Never click on links in email, unless you know exactly
what it is. Always use bookmarks or type in bank or
other important web sites.

The Work: Be aware of links in email

Difficulty: 1

The Need: Do – well in this case don't do….

20 DON'T UNSUBSCRIBE FROM THAT JUNK MAIL

When you start looking at some of that junk email, you may see a link at the bottom that says "click here to unsubscribe".

Don't click on that link!

Usually the only thing clicking on that link does is let the bad guys know they have a real email address to send more junk to.

The best thing to do is add that message to your spam folder and let Google, Microsoft, or whoever filter the mail. That's why I recommend having multiple email addresses.

You can unsubscribe to mail that you know where it comes from. If you bought something online or gave your email to a store like JC Penny's, they will send you advertising mail. If you don't want email from them anymore, you can click on their unsubscribe links and they will remove you from their list. It usually takes a couple weeks to be removed from these lists.

If it is a legitimate company and especially if you signed up for the mails by buying something then you can feel safe in unsubscribing.

***

Recommendation: Don't "unsubscribe" from that Viagra junk email, it will just generate more junk mail.

The Work: Don't be tempted to click on "unsubscribe" in junk mail.

Difficulty: 0

The Need: Do – or again, don't do.

21 DON'T USE ADOBE FLASH

Adobe Flash Player is used to play many videos on the internet. Or at least it used to be....

Today's internet has advanced to where it plays video directly through the web page using HTML 5. HTML is just the language that web pages are written in. Even YouTube defaults to playing video through HTML 5 now, not *Flash*.

In chapter 5 I mentioned how *Flash* was becoming outdated and even the source of many a security holes for virus and malware. *Adobe* even seemed to concede this in late 2015 they issued news of the launch of a new product to play media on the internet and the discontinuation of *Flash* while I was writing this book.

YouTube stopped using *Flash* a couple years ago and *Apple* has never liked it. Steve Jobs wrote on Apples web site that *Flash* was "..vulnerable to exploits, crash-prone, and incapable of performing well on mobile devices." When the *iPhone* and *iPad* took off, nether one supporting *Flash*, the internet started to change to work on these devices.

Google Chrome has its own version of a flash player built in and secured. So if you visit a website that needs flash, Chrome is your best option.

Firefox still uses Flash, but it is turned off by default, so you can click on a video to watch when you want to.

Adobe's Flash player has been a known security risk for years. Virus or malware makers target *Flash* as their way into your computer. The reason you see *Flash* updating so much is for them to fix the "holes". Many of today's ads are still Flash based, and if they are infected you may not even need to click on it. Flash video plays automatically by default and it can let in an infection.

You can choose not to install flash on a new computer or uninstall it from your current computer. You can use the internet and watch all the cat videos you need without having Flash installed on your computer.

The only sites you may really need *Flash* or *Java* for are some gaming sites. For them I suggest trying *Chrome* first, then if they will not run correctly go to *Firefox* with *Flash* installed.

HOW TO UNINSTALL FLASH

Click on the Start menu > type the words "uninstall program". You should see "uninstall a program" or "change and remove programs" in the search box. Just look for flash in the list in that window. Click the "uninstall" option to the right or double click the Flash line to start the uninstall process. Follow the prompts.

***

Recommendation: Don't use Adobe Flash. You can probably even uninstall it. Try *Chrome* first, then go to *Firefox* with *Flash* installed if needed.

The Work: Uninstalling *Flash*

Difficultly: 1

The Need: Should do.

22 DON'T USE JAVA

As mentioned in chapter 5, *Java* is another one of the programs that the bad guys target for a way to get into your computer. Even without "security holes", *Java* can be used to damage or infect your computer just by sending you a Java program in an email link or download. **Remember don't click on links in emails!**

Java, like *Adobe Flash,* is pretty much outdated. It is not used in most web sites anymore. The main exception to this is online gaming sites such as Pogo.com. These gaming sites don't want to spend too much money or effort to change their sites to more modern HTML 5, so they still may require *Java* and often *Flash* too.

Some older programs used *Java* also, but like the web modern programs do not.

If you ever come to a site or program that does need *Java* – and it is one you really want or need – it will offer to install *Java* for you. Like Chapter 13 advises, if you are prompted to install *Java* or anything you're not 100% sure you want. Say NO

You should be able to use the internet just fine; minus these gaming sites without *Java* installed on your computer.

So if you do not visit online gaming sites often, you can uninstall *Java* from your computer.

If you do visit Pogo.com or other gaming sites and need *Java* then you can keep it.

HOW TO UNINSTALL JAVA

Click on the Start menu > type the words "uninstall program". You should see "uninstall a program" or "change and remove programs" in the search box. Just look for Java in the list in that window. Click the "uninstall" option to the right or double click the Java line to start the uninstall process. Follow the prompts.

You may even have more than one version. If so, uninstall each one.

Now your computer has one less program you don't need, and it removes some security issues.

***

Recommendation: Uninstall *Java*. You don't need it for 99% of the internet.

The Work: uninstalling *Java*.

Difficulty: 1

The Need: Should do.

23 USE A VPN

Have you heard of a VPN (Virtual Private Network) perhaps on TV or the movies? If you watch any of the *NCIS* TV shows you have. Abby and MaGee talk about them all the time.

I won't get too technical but a VPN lets you connect to the internet (or your work computer) through a special "tunnel" that no one else can see into. By tunnel I mean think of a tunnel you drive through a mountain, but it is your own tunnel no one else can use. You are the only car on the road. So for the internet connection, you are the only person using this connection.

A VPN can have many "privacy" benefits for people who are worried about web sites and government tracking them. You can research those if you like.

*While writing this book, there was a news story about a reporter being "spied on" while using a public Wi-Fi from an airline. So using a VPN is becoming more important in public places.

I strongly recommend a VPN for laptop users who connect to any free wireless networks like coffee shops or hotels. These are the places where someone can use that connection to "snoop" on what you are doing. They can watch you shop and what you do on Facebook, and if they are really trying, they can set up a fake connection to bank sites or a key logger to get your passwords.

I am including the VPN option just because I mainly want you to be aware of the option to surf privately. Not everyone needs one, and it needs some setup and confidence in your computer skills

Setting up the VPN is becoming easier all the time. If you have read this far into the book you can do it.

TIP: don't use coffee shops or hotels to connect to banking or credit card sites without a VPN unless absolutely necessary. If you are traveling, your smart phone can do anything you need to do with your bank using their app.

There are free and paid VPN services available. A free VPN program or VPN add-on to your web browser should be fine for most users. The paid services offer faster speed guarantees and options like connecting to foreign countries.

Free VPN's: proXPN

               Hotspot Shield. Browser plug in. (ad supported)

Paid VPN's: proXPN, PureVPN

Whenever you go someplace public simply start the VPN service before you open your browser.

***

Recommendation: Use a VPN on free Wi-Fi spots like coffee shops or hotels.

The Work: Installing the program, turning on the VPN.

Difficulty: 2

Need: Can do, especially if you use a laptop at free Wi-Fi like coffee shops or hotels often.

24 USE NOSCRIPT WITH FIREFOX

In chapter 7 I suggested using an add-on to block ads. The add-on for ad blocking at least partially worked by blocking small programs run in the web browser called *scripts*.

A more advanced add-on for the *Firefox* web browser is called *NoScript*. *NoScript* will block pretty much all scripts on a web page; only allowing the very basic parts of a web page to show. Therefor protecting you almost 100% from any bad ads, pop ups, redirects, hijacking, virus, or malware from being installed without YOU specifically downloading and installing it.

The reason I did not mention it in chapter 7 and am including it in a later chapter is that by it blocking all scripts it essentially breaks every web page. As mentioned, the way the web works today; most pages need to use JavaScript, as well as other elements not directly part of the HTML or the base web site.

By installing *NoScript* almost no web site will work correctly, if at all. Facebook will not load at all; it shows an error message saying you need JavaScript enabled. Other web sites like MSN don't display right. With Facebook being the most used web site today, and to some IS the internet, just installing and using no script makes no sense.

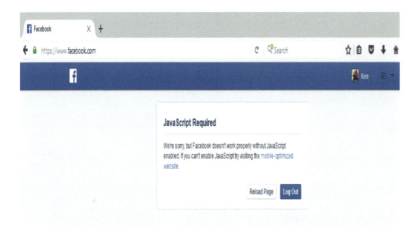

Facebook with NoScript

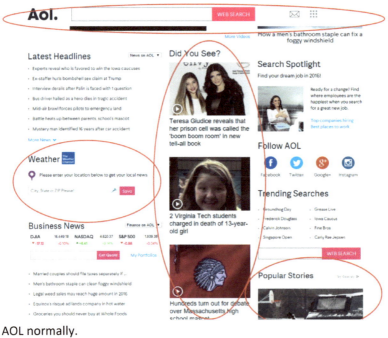

AOL normally.

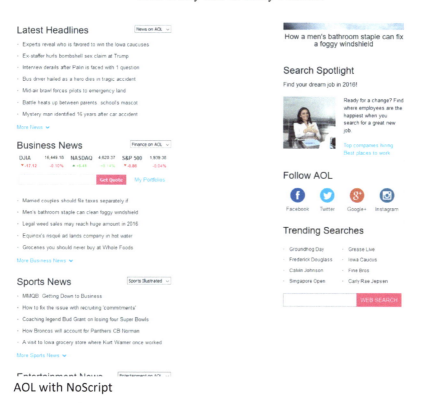

AOL with NoScript

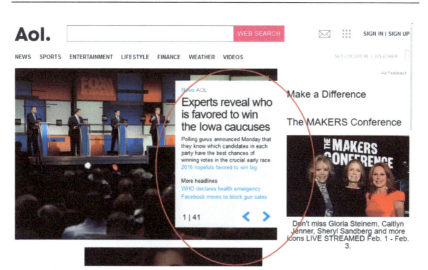

AOL with NoScript, top stories don't move *and* you can't click to the next story.

Here AOL is mostly usable, except you can't change the top stories, so you would have to allow use the NoScript menu to allow some of the blocked content.

NoScript needs to be taught what web pages or ***parts of web pages*** to block. Did you notice that last part? *NoScript* can just block parts of a web page or site.

Noscript will show you what parts or scripts it is blocking, and you can tell it not to block one or more of them until the website works correctly.

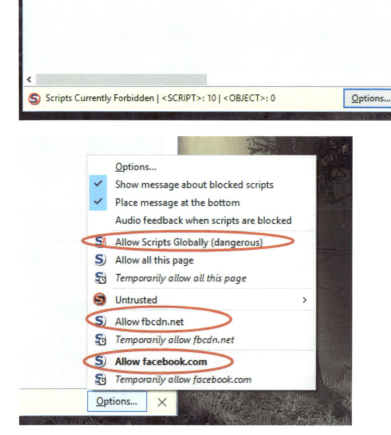

I won't lie; this process of telling *NoScript* to unblock a site or parts of a site is very annoying.

Remember EVERY site you visit will need some kind of tweaking to the *NoScript* settings!

Now, you may think "I only visit a couple sites". Well, as I think I said somewhere earlier in the book, you visit more sites than you think you do. You visit online banking sites, news, shopping, video, look at photos, and every link you click on at Facebook, Yahoo, MSN, or AOL could take you to a totally different web site to read the article. So you would be looking at a site that doesn't look right or an error message on every click until you tell *NoScript* what to do.

This gets very annoying; especially the first few days when every site needs the configuration done. NoScript will remember your choice and in the future you will not need to configure it again.

I will confess, I don't use Noscript because *I* could not put up with all the configuring I had to do. Now I definitely visit a lot of different web sites, doing research, so I am not a good example.

I am including NoScript as a suggestion for the people who for whatever reason need the best protection on web sites. It is the best *free* way to almost 100% protect yourself from the ways of getting infected besides directly downloading and installing malware manually.

NoScript is only available for *Firefox*. There are a couple similar add-ons for *Chrome*, but I don't believe they are as easy to use or as effective.

✳✳✳

Recommendation: Use *Firefox* and install the *NoScript* add-on.

The Work: Installing an add-on, and training NoScript for each website.

Difficulty: 3

The Need: Can do.

25 USE SANDBOXIE

In chapter 24 I mentioned that using *NoScript* was the best FREE way to protect your computer from getting infected. Another way to protect your computer is to use a program called *Sandboxie* that can separate your online activity from the rest of the computer. If you get an infection, you simply delete everything and start over again.

Sandboxie creates a container placed around an application running within Windows, very much like a VPN (chapter 23) creates a "tunnel" for your internet connection. Both of these keep what you're doing from being seen by other people or from the rest of the computer in *Sanboxie*'s case. So when you're online your browser and internet connection is kept totally separate from the rest of your computer. If you download something bad it can't install on to your computer. If something bad enough affects your browser or the *Sandboxie* work space, you can delete it and start over again.

Sandboxie is one program of a group that creates this "sandbox" inside your computer. That is how they get their name. Sandboxie is the only one of these programs I am familiar with and know is recommended. You can search for others and for more details on how sandbox programs work if you like.

From Sanboxie's web site:

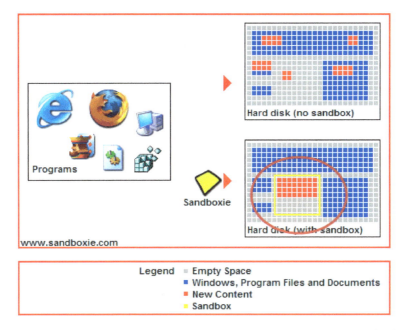

This shows how the data in red, goes into a separate space on the hard drive than the rest of the data of your computer.

Sandboxie costs $20 a year or $35 for a lifetime license. It also has a free trial.

If you are someone who has had a lot of bad experiences with getting virus or malware infections and think you need to take drastic steps to protect yourself, you can check into Sandboxie.

Tip: Try to save your bookmarks so you will have them if you have to delete and redo your sandbox.

***

Recommendation: Install and use Sandboxie if you think you need to protect yourself from virus or malware infections in an extreme way.

The Work: Installing, setting up, and learning how to use Sandboxie

Difficulty: 3

The Need: Can do.

26 USE HTTPS EVERYWHERE PLUGIN

I hope you know that when you are shopping, banking, or doing anything online that is supposed to be "secure", to look for the https at the front of the website address in the address bar. The https area should also be green. The S being the big thing to look for. It means that the site you are on is using a SECURE and encrypted connection. So whatever you send to that site - be it credit card number or bank account log on- that information *can not* be seen by someone "watching" your internet traffic. i.e. shopping at amazon from a coffee shop. (Don't do this without a VPN from chapter 23).

That S in https, makes online shopping and banking more secure than handing your credit card to your waiter or cahier. That S makes sure that information is safe. While a person who walks to another room to run your credit card can copy it in no time flat. You even see news reports of peoples credit cards being copied by a "skimmer" at ATM's or gas stations.

Any site you visit that needs a log on or handles credit cards is going to be https. Unless you visit some very shady places and are willing to give your credit card number to anyone who asks... (I hope not from reading this far into the book.)

The HTTPS Everywhere ad-on for Chrome and Firefox will make the connection secure by directing you to the correct page, or warn you about being on an unsecure page.

The problem this can help with is even if a websites log on is https, the rest of their page may not be. It will make as much of the whole site https as is supported by the site. This is an added anonymizing privacy feature. i.e. no one will be able to "see" any part of the site that supports the https connection.

Another thing HTTPS Everywhere can help warn you if you get malware or go to a bad website, or click in an email link (per chapter 19, don't do that) and they are trying to trick you into getting your card number. As mentioned earlier in the book the bad guys can make web pages that look exactly like your bank or credit card, or even Amazon. OR you could click on an old link to a site that should be https and is not.

This will not make everything you do https secure!

Not all websites are supported and if parts of the site don't allow https, those will still be visible.

For example the images on a site may not be https. So people could "see" that your web browser downloaded those images.

HTTPS Everywhere is made by The Tor (Browser) Project and the Electronic Frontier Foundation. So this is a trustworthy ad-on.

There is a push in the internet community for everything to be https. I think in just a couple years this will be the case.

This is just another optional add-on that can help you feel safer knowing that as much of your web browsing is not being watched as possible.

I currently do not use HTTPS Everywhere. I know the sites I visit are secure when I need them to be for shopping, and for just normal browsing I don't care if sites are not encrypted.

I have suggested A LOT of add-ons in this book; you probably don't want to use them all. This would be my least suggested. As mentioned above, as long as you don't visit too crazy a site and know to look for https when you buy something online (and have an ad blocker?) you should be fine. See chapter 30 for my must have list of add-ons.

***

Recommendation: Use the HTTPS Everywhere ad-on to make sure as much of your internet browsing is not being seen as possible – if you want to.

The Work: Install the add-on

Difficulty: 1

The Need: Can do.

27 USE THE TOR BROWSER

One thing some people want to do is browse the internet "anonymously". This means no one can watch or tell where you have been on the internet; if they watch your internet traffic, leave "unwanted" cookies on your computer, or even know "where" you are when you go online. This means blocking targeted ads as well as help people who are worried about the government or businesses knowing too much about you. (personal privacy).

Visiting web sites lets those sites know all kinds of information about you, like where you are (city and state), see other web sites you have visited, and some fear even more personal information. It has been shown that some web sites can know if you are a man or a woman, your general health; – have you looked up that weird mark you found on your arm or other symptoms of a disease?, and (very scary to some) even if someone is gay or straight.

So there is a big push for people to be able to surf the web and not worry about "someone" knowing too much information about them (you) just by being on the internet.

Enter the *Tor Browser*. The *Tor Browser* is another web browser like *Chrome* or *Firefox*; in fact it is based on the *Firefox* base code. *Tor Browser* was designed to protect you from all of these issues by providing you with an IP address that's not from you're service provider and does not keep cookies.

It is essentially the *Firefox* browser, which is open source, with some customizing done with add-ons like I've mentioned in this book already installed. (to keep it simple).

From the torproject.org website

Notice how it resembles Firefox

Since the *Tor Browser* is more – less just another internet browser, you can simply download and install it. Then use it like normal *Firefox* with the added security of being more anonymous.

So if you are worried about your insurance company increasing your healthcare cost because you visit some health web sites or you don't like the idea of every website knowing where you are you can use the *Tor Browser*.

The downside: without certain cookies or your location some web sites don't always work right; like Google maps.

I have this in the advanced section because using the ad blockers from chapter 7 will be enough for most people. But there is absolutely no harm in trying the *Tor Browser* and if you don't like it you can stop using it or uninstall it.

***

Recommendation: Try the *Tor Browser* if you have personal privacy concerns. Don't forget to use a VPN from chapter 23 if you do have privacy concerns.

The Work: Installing a new browser.

Difficulty: 1

The Need: Can do.

28 ENCRYPT YOUR HARD DRIVE

Like VPNs from chapter 23, if you watch NCIS or any crime based TV you have heard of encrypting a hard drive. Again Abby and McGee talk about it almost every week. From those shows you may understand that encrypting a hard drive makes it unreadable to anyone who steels, try's to use, or even takes apart a computer. Of course Abby and the NSA could get that data within the 1hr TV show. In reality the police or even the NSA would not be able to get into the hard drive for weeks or months – if at all. Any police or government agency would need a warrant to get the decryption information from the encrypting software company – if there is one.

Without getting too deep into any conspiracy theories, if your hard drive is encrypted; NO ONE is getting information off of it.

This is included in the advanced section because most people **do not need this** yet, it definitely takes some set up, and you could lose everything if you forget your password (or something goes wrong). I am just making you aware that it is an option.

If you have a "Pro" version of Windows or higher you have the ability to encrypt your hard drive with no extra software. Simply click on your Start button and type the word "BitLocker". You should see an option to open *BitLocker* or the *BitLocker* control panel. For more information visit

Microsofts web site http://windows.microsoft.com/en-us/windows/protect-files-bitlocker-drive-encryption

If you have a Mac with OS X Lion or later, and a working OS X Recovery volume on your startup disk, you can use FileVault. FileVault is turned on in the Security & Privacy pane of System Preferences. For more information visit Apples web site https://support.apple.com/en-us/HT204837

There are other companies that offer disk encryption if you don't have an eligible OS or don't want to use the one from Microsoft or Apple.

TrueCrypt has been the free open source standard for years. It has recently stopped development (2015) for some mysterious reason. Really, one day they just shutdown with no warning. They mention on their web site that it is no longer safe, but do not give any examples or proof. Some suggest that the government either wanted or found a way to decrypt their data. So the developers decided to stop the project rather than "break" it. There is no proof of this. In fact TrueCrypt has since been tested and found to have no serious flaws. Many die-hard fans are sticking with it.

An off shoot of *TrueCrypt* is *VeraCrypt*. It uses the base code of *TrueCrypt* but is still being supported and developed. It is also open source and tested. So this is the software I will suggest if you want or need to encrypt your hard drive and not use the one from Microsoft or Apple.

*Since I consider this VERY ADVANCED, **don't try drive encryption** unless you think you really need it or are told to use it by work, AND ARE VERY CONFIDENT IN YOUR COMPUTER USAGE SKILLS.
If you need it for work, they should set it up for you.

***

Recommendation: Use encryption only if you think it is really necessary. Use your OS's encryption or VeraCrypt.

The Work: Learning more about drive encryption, backing up your data, installing and setting up the encryption.

Difficulty: 10

The Need: Can do - only if necessary.

29 FUTURE TIP – INTERNET OF THINGS

A new buzz word that has come about in the past few years is the Internet Of Things (IOT). This refers to all the other things that can connect to the internet other than computers, phone, and tables.

These things are refrigerators, thermostats, doorbells, cars, and even (yes) lightbulbs. TV's probably count too. You may have seen or heard about thermostats that do this now. They are "smart" thermostats that can adjust themselves based on your usage, and you can connect to them from your computer or phone. A connected refrigerator has been a dream of manufacturers since the 1960's.

The Kitchen of the Future from the 1960's

Today connected everything is becoming a reality.

The problem this is going to cause is, **the more things connected to the internet, the more things that can be hacked.**

There is already news that the lightbulbs, thermostats, and doorbells that already exist have already been hacked; or at least holes have been found and fixed.

My *Future Tip* to you is if you ever get these IOT devices; connect them to the Guest network on your router and say NO to allowing that Guest network from accessing other devices on the main network.

In the future, routers may include a special connection similar to the Guest network just for these IOT devices. But for now I can just give you a heads up on how to set up these IOT devices to help protect someone from using them to hack into your home network.

*While writing this book security expert Steve Gibson released information on how to secure IOT devices and suggests to be completely safe, you would need 3 different routers.   ***

***

Recommendation: Use the Guest network for other things connected to internet like door bells, thermostats, and lightbulbs. *Do research on newest security thoughts on IOT devices if you start to get a "smart home".

The Work: Need to make sure the Guest network is set up on router, and not allowed to connect to devices on the main network.

Difficulty: 2

The Need: Future, unless you are an early adopter of internet connected light bulbs.

30 SUMMARY

You don't need to use all of the suggestions in this book. In fact, if you did you would probably not be able to use the internet very quickly or comfortably. Using all the add-ons I mention can slow down your browser. Using the add-ons, a vpn, and tor browser would make it almost impossible to use the internet. So you need to choose what suggestions you need or would help you the most.

I organized the chapters / suggestions in pretty much the order of importance. With the last chapters being more information that these advanced options exist, but not thinking most people need them.

The first chapters are things everyone should do.

Each chapter ends with a "NEED" category to help you know how important I think it is. If the NEED is "DO", it is something I think everyone should do. These will be something like passwords, password managers, ad blockers, and so on.

Here are the chapters suggestions that I recommend you review and make sure are part of your security habit. They will not interfere with each other and make up the least you should do to protect yourself. If you follow all or most of these, you should have little to worry about while using the internet.

Chapter 1 : Backup Your Files
Chapter 2 : Put a Password on Your Computer
Chapter 3 : Create a Standard User Account
Chapter 4 : Antivirus and Malware Protection
Chapter 5 : Keep Your Computer and Software Updated
Chapter 6 : Use a Better Browser
Chapter 7 : Use an Ad Blocker
Chapter 8 : Use Strong Passwords!
Chapter 9 : Use a Password Manager
Chapter 11 : Use 2 Factor Authentication
Chapter 13: Pay Attention to Pop ups
Chapter 15: Beware of Extra Software Installs
Chapter 21: Don't Use Adobe Flash

Becoming more important as I am writing this book -
Chapter 23 : Use a VPN (If you use public Wi-Fi)

Wow, that's 14 chapters, half the book I consider necessary for everyone to do for good internet security. No wonder my couple page pamphlet ended up turning into a book. Even if I remove a couple that may be a little less important, that's at least 10 things you need to think about that most people probably don't.

31 BACK IT UP, BACK IT UP, BACK IT UP

Backing up your files is the most important thing you should do. Backing up is so important that I am reminding you several times. This is the last chapter / reminder of the book to back up your files.

If you don't back up your data now, I hope your computer crashes tomorrow and you lose everything. (Just kidding.....kinda)

ABOUT THE AUTHOR

Ken Barker is a computer technician who has been working on computers for over 10 years. He has worked at Staples and several local computer shops and software companies. He has worked customer support / customer service for most of his life.

Customers always comment on how good Ken is with talking to them and explaining computer / technology stuff in a way they can understand and not be condescending or make them feel stupid.

Ken also runs a technology news site called TechBreakdown.tv where he tries to convey technology news and information in a way that the average person can understand it.

www.ingramcontent.com/pod-product-compliance
Lightning Source LLC
Chambersburg PA
CBHW041142050326
40689CB00001B/446